EXCHANGE RISK AND CORPORATE INTERNATIONAL FINANCE

EXCHANGE RISK AND CORPORATE INTERNATIONAL FINANCE

Robert Z. Aliber

A HALSTED PRESS BOOK

John Wiley & Sons
New York

First published 1978 by
THE MACMILLAN PRESS LTD
London and Basingstoke

*Published in the U.S.A
by Halsted Press, a Division
of John Wiley & Sons, Inc.
New York.*

Printed in Great Britain

Library of Congress Cataloging in Publication Data
Aliber, Robert Z.
Exchange risk and corporate international finance.

"A Halsted Press book."
Includes index.
1. International business enterprises—Finance.
2. Foreign exchange problem. I. Title.
HG4028.I53A35   1978   658.1'5   78–4645
ISBN 0–470–26307–5

Contents

Contents

List of Tables and Figures

Acknowledgements

Work began on this book several years ago in an attempt to understand better the implications for business firms of some of the developments in our understanding of macro-international financial relationships. Moreover, the various propositions developed in the theory of finance for a closed economy had not yet been extended to the open international economy.

Discussions with colleagues and with students have been helpful. I am especially grateful for the comments and suggestions of Rolf Banz, Donna Bean, Christine R. Hekman, Richard S. Karplus, Richard M. Levich, John Redmond, and Thomas S. Wurster. This book has gone through N drafts; the patience and forbearance of Fran Miller, Patty Pazera and Joy Ritchie have been greatly appreciated.

R.Z.A.

Part I

1. Introduction

The major sources of financial uncertainty for firms engaged in international business arise from changes in exchange rates and changes in exchange controls – events which are not readily predictable. The risks of changes in exchange rates – both of changes in parities under a pegged rate system and fluctuations under a floating rate system – are inherent in a system of national currencies, just as the risks of changes in exchange controls and of expropriation are inherent in a system of multiple sovereigns.

Changes in exchange rates and in exchange controls may have a dramatic impact on the profits of individual firms, their net worth, market values, and their competitive positions in foreign markets as well as domestic markets. Some firms have reported declines in net earnings attributable to changes in exchange rates of $50 or $60 million; others have reported gains. The impacts on profits can be so sharp that managements frequently attempt to arrange the financial structures of the firms to minimise any adverse effect. The choice of currency of denomination for import and export transactions, of countries in which to locate new plants, and of the centres in which these activities are to be financed are affected by anticipation of such changes. So is their choice of centres in which to hold financial assets. Finally, the calculation of income, and hence of tax liabilities, is affected by the exchange rates used to convert foreign currency values into dollars.[1]

The managers of the firms must determine when to hold long positions in particular currencies and when those positions should be increased or reduced. Changes in the currency mix of the firm's assets and liabilities may incur costs – and someone must decide when it is worthwhile to incur these costs.

Some countries use exchange controls to delay or prevent the repatriation of profits, capital or sales receipts from the subsidiaries located in their jurisdictions to their foreign parents. The application of exchange controls places firms at a disadvantage, and they try to minimise losses that result from these controls. Attempting to minimise these losses may incur costs. Some countries have expropriated the local

3

ownership interests of foreign firms with less than complete compensation; as a result, the net worth of these firms may decline. The managers must decide how to minimise the likelihood of these losses – and whether the possible costs incurred are too high.

Changes in exchange rates and in exchange controls result from the interplay of national and international economics and politics. Governments are constantly seeking to advance their interests and the interests of their constituents; variations in money supply growth, exchange rates and exchange controls are part of the maximising process. The managers of firms seek to protect and enhance their firms' financial interests – they want to increase profits and yet avoid sharp losses that might result if changes in exchange rates occur. The timing of these changes must be anticipated, and the currency mix of the firm's financial structure arranged to minimise both the losses from these changes and the costs incurred to avoid these losses. The managers must decide when it is preferable to denominate trade and investment transactions in dollars and when in foreign currencies; they must decide when the expansion of foreign subsidiaries should be financed by borrowing in dollars and when in foreign currencies – and which foreign currencies.

The managers may be able to avoid or reduce the risks of losses from changes in exchange controls if the risks can be sold to others. The buyers of these risks, however, seek appropriate reimbursement. And so considerable value is attached to the appropriate estimate of these risks.

Various sources provide advice about how the firms should evaluate their exposure to losses from changes in exchange rates and exchange controls. Accountants indicate how the changes in exchange rates affect the income and net worth. Banks buy and sell foreign exchange, and suggest how individual transactions should be financed. This advice is subject to several shortcomings. The information developed by the accountants to provide information on the firm's performance is not immediately appropriate for deciding how the firm's income and net worth will be affected by changes in exchange rates. The advice offered by bankers frequently ignores the systematic relationship between changes in the exchange rates and the interest rates on similar assets and liabilities denominated in different currencies.

THE SCOPE OF THIS BOOK

This book provides a framework for the systematic analysis of the financial risks of international business. The concepts of exchange risk and political risk are related to the structures of the international financial and sovereignty systems. These concepts are examined with the use of extensive data on changes in exchange rates, changes in national commodity price levels, and interest rates on similar assets denominated in various currencies. The recommendations of professional accounting groups about the estimation of the firm's exposure to these risks are examined in terms of these concepts and data. The implications of alternative strategies that the firm might take towards these risks are also evaluated in terms of these relationships. The assumption throughout is that the firm is risk averse – it wishes to minimise the variations in its income that might result from unanticipated changes in exchange rates and exchange controls.

The book does not indicate how the corporate treasurers should structure the currency mix of the firm's assets and liabilities; rather, it provides a framework for analysis of this problem. Moreover, the orientation is not towards technique – there are no instructions on how to buy and sell foreign exchange, or how to deal with exchange control authorities; rather the emphasis is on concepts and framework.

Part I focuses on the macro-characteristics. of the international financial system. Chapter 2 examines changes in exchange rates in terms of the structure of the international financial system. The logical systematic relationships among changes in exchange rates, interest rates on similar assets denominated in various currencies, and changes in national price levels are considered in Chapter 3. Chapter 4 discusses political risk, i.e. the risk that the authorities of the state will intervene between borrower and lender and delay or prevent the fulfilment of the contracts.

Three chapters summarise the relevant data for the concepts noted in Chapters 3 and 4. Chapter 5 considers data relating changes in exchange rates to changes in national price levels. The data on relationships between interest rates on similar assets denominated in various currencies and changes in spot exchange rates are noted in Chapter 6. Chapter 7 discusses the relationship between the interest rates on similar assets denominated in various currencies and forward exchange rates, as well as between the interest rates on similar assets produced in domestic and in offshore markets.

Part II provides a framework for organising the firm's decisions about altering its exposure to exchange risk. Chapter 8 examines the alternative ways in which a firm might alter its exposure to exchange and political risk and the costs of using these alternatives. The alternative ways of estimating the firm's exposure to losses and gains from changes in exchange rates and how the firm's net worth and income are affected by such changes, both in the short run and the long run, are discussed in Chapter 9. The tax implications of losses and gains attributable to changes in exchange rates are discussed in Chapter 10. Chapter 11 evaluates a set of strategies that the firm might take towards these risks. Chapter 12 provides a comprehensive view of the firm's exposure to loss from changes in exchange rates and exchange controls.

SOURCES

Several texts provide extensive descriptive material about various aspects of international business finance. See David K. Eiteman and Arthur I. Stonehill, *Multinational Business Finance* (Reading, Mass.: Addison-Wesley, 1973); J. Fred Weston and Bart W. Sorge, *International Managerial Finance* (Homewood, Ill.: Richard D. Irwin, 1972). Various case-oriented texts also deal in part with the exchange risk; see David B. Zenoff and Jack Zwick, *International Financial Management* (Englewood Cliffs, N.J.: Prentice-Hall, 1969). For empirical material on the financial behaviour of various multinational firms, see Sidney M. Robbins and Robert B. Stobaugh, *Money in the Multinational Enterprise* (New York: Basic Books, 1973).

2. Changes in Exchange Rates as Economic Disturbances

Changes in exchange rates are uncertain events. Most changes in exchange rates are associated with differential movements in national price levels – the price levels in the countries whose currencies are devalued or depreciate have risen more rapidly than the U.S. price level and, to a lesser extent, the countries whose currencies were revalued or appreciated have had less rapid inflation. Even then, the timing of such changes cannot be foretold with accuracy. Moreover, not all changes in exchange rates, especially on a month-to-month or quarter-to-quarter basis, reflect changes in relative prices. Since most industrial countries ceased pegging their currencies in early 1973, the exchange rate between the mark price of the U.S. dollar has fluctuated sharply, even though the U.S. and German price levels have increased at almost the same rate.

The frequency of changes in the price of the U.S. dollar in terms of other currencies since 1948 is summarised in Table 2.1. Changes in rates in the years since 1967 were more frequent than in the previous decade. Depreciations have usually been much more frequent than appreciations except in 1971, 1973, and 1974. In the 1950s and 1960s the median change in parities was very large, frequently more than 50 per cent. In 1962, for example, Israel devalued by 67 per cent, while in 1965 the Philippines devalued by 95 per cent. These large changes in parities generally involved countries which account for a small part of total U.S. trade.

When the change in the price of the U.S. dollar in terms of each country's currency is weighted by the country's importance in total U.S. trade, the annual change in the price of the dollar in terms of all other currencies averages to less than 2 per cent a year. In only one year, 1949, did the change exceed 10 per cent, and in only one other year, 1975, the change exceeded 5 per cent. In 1967 when Britain, Spain and many other countries devalued their currencies, the increase in the trade-weighted value of the dollar was less than 4 per cent.

7

TABLE 2.1 Changes in the Foreign Exchange Value of the U.S. Dollar

	Percentage increase in trade-weighted dollar		Number of changes in excess of 3 per cent	
Year	Annual	Cumulative	Appreciations	Depreciations
1949	16.08	16.08	2	113
1950	2.82	18.90	3	9
1951	0.08	18.98	2	4
1952	−0.89	18.09	3	4
1953	2.20	20.29	1	8
1954	4.22	24.51	1	6
1955	2.91	27.42	1	8
1956	−0.67	26.75	2	3
1957	2.66	29.41	1	35
1958	2.57	31.98	1	39
1959	0.73	32.71	2	9
1960	1.39	32.10	1	7
1961	2.66	36.76	3	8
1962	3.40	40.16	0	10
1963	1.10	41.26	0	5
1964	3.47	44.73	0	8
1965	1.41	46.14	0	8
1966	1.08	47.22	0	7
1967	3.74	50.96	0	46
1968	1.00	51.96	0	6
1969	0.12	52.08	1	31
1970	−0.22	51.86	1	10
1971	−3.68	48.18	104	16
1972	0.30	48.48	14	35
1973	−2.57	45.91	105	7
1974	0.71	46.62	57	24
1975	7.46	54.08	1	83
1976	4.44	58.52	14	78

Source: *Direction of Trade*, International Monetary Fund, annual 1968–72.
Note: Trade weights are based on 1968 U.S. imports and exports.

These changes in exchange rates reflect the interplay of national monetary policies, and the juxtaposition of these policies with changes in the international financial system, especially with the arrangements for producing international monies.

The increased frequency of changes in exchange rates in recent years leads to the question of whether, in the next five or ten years, countries will retain floating exchange rates or whether they will again peg their currencies. The answer is unclear, although exchange rates appear likely to vary more frequently than in the 1960s, and central bank intervention with floating rates may be more extensive than in the last several years.

This chapter first considers the essential features of the alternative exchange rate systems, and the impact of domestic monetary policies on these systems. Then non-monetary sources of changes in exchange rates are discussed.

THE EXCHANGE MARKET ARRANGEMENTS

In a world with two or more currencies, a foreign exchange market is necessary. National monies are not perfect substitutes for each other; each serves as an acceptable means of payment in only a limited geographic area, usually congruent with established national boundaries. The key questions about the organisation of the foreign exchange market involve the frequency with which exchange rates change, and the mechanisms by which these changes occur.

In a few instances the price of one unit of country A's currency is unalterably set in terms of one unit of country B's currency as long as the existing set of institutional arrangements is unchanged; the exchange rate is fixed.[1] Examples include the relationships between the Luxembourg franc and the Belgian franc, and between the Panamanian dollar and the U.S. dollar. Luxembourg and Panama have their own coins but neither has a currency of its own; Luxembourg uses the Belgian currency and Panama, U.S. currency. Until each develops its own central bank and its own national money, its exchange rate will remain fixed.

The alternative to fixed rates is flexible rates, either continuously floating rates or periodically adjustable rates, e.g. pegged rates. Under a floating rate system, the price of foreign monies in terms of domestic money rises and falls in response to changes in supply and demand. Intervention by the monetary authorities in the foreign exchange market is permissible; some central banks buy and sell their currencies to limit the day-to-day or week-to-week movements in exchange rates, or to influence the direction or magnitude of the changes in the price of their currencies. Central bank intervention policies have differed; the Bank of Japan has intervened extensively, the Bank of England sporadically, the Bundesbank modestly.

Most currencies have been pegged for the last twenty-five years and, indeed, for most of the last century. While the major industrial countries permitted their currencies to float in March 1973, most other currencies remained pegged.

A pegged rate system has two essential components. One is the parity, par value or central value – the price of an international unit of account, such as gold or the dollar, in terms of the standard unit of the national currency, such as the peso or the pound sterling.[2] The Mexican peso had a parity of 12.5 pesos to the U.S. dollar from 1954 to 1976, while the pound sterling had a parity of $2.80 from 1949 to 1967.

The second essential component of the pegged rate system is the set of support limits to the deviation of the actual exchange rate from the parity; the central bank is obliged, either by international agreement or self-imposed commitment, to prevent the market exchange rate from moving beyond these limits. These limits have ranged from several tenths of 1 per cent either side of the parity to about 2 per cent. Each central bank keeps the price of its currency from moving beyond the support limits by buying and selling its money in the exchange market. The market exchange rate may differ from the parity within the support limits; in effect, the currency floats within a narrow band between these limits. A pegged rate with extremely wide support limits is effectively a floating rate.

A floating rate system might seem more 'natural' than a pegged rate system, since the currency will float unless the authorities peg the rate. Tradition may explain why central banks peg their currencies. National currencies were indirectly pegged to each other when countries pegged their currencies to gold. Beyond tradition, some monetary authorities believe that large variations in the price of foreign exchange in terms of their currencies deter international trade and investment. The authorities in countries in which the ratio of foreign trade to national income is relatively high believe that the costs to their national economies from the smaller volume of trade and investment exceed the benefits otherwise associated with floating rates.

Some countries permit their currencies to float because they are uncertain about the appropriate value for a new parity when the old one no longer seems appropriate; the floating rate is viewed as an interim arrangement. In 1969, for example, Germany permitted the mark to float for about two weeks in the belief that market forces would suggest the value at which the mark should again be pegged.

Some monetary authorities, especially in very large countries, favour a floating exchange rate system because they believe that they then have greater scope to follow desired monetary and fiscal policies; they are not obliged to design their financial policies to maintain the foreign exchange value of their currencies at particular values, as under a pegged rate system. Another advantage attributed to a floating rate system is that changes in the demands for imports and exports have a smaller impact on domestic prices, incomes and employment than under a pegged rate system because any tendency towards payments imbalances is neutralised through changes in exchange rates.

During much of the 1945–70 period, adherence to the pegged rate system was viewed as a commitment to exchange parities at particular values; the exchange rate structure was more pegged than adjustable. National monetary authorities were reluctant to alter their monetary and fiscal policies to attain payments balance at the existing parities. As the need to reduce payments imbalances became pressing, they altered access of traders and investors to the foreign exchange market by manipulating tariffs, licences to buy foreign exchange, and import deposit requirements; the generic term for such measures is exchange controls. The variety of such controls is extensive and includes taxes, such as the U.S. Interest Equalisation Tax, and moral suasion measures, such as 'Buy America' and 'See America First'. Exporters may be required to sell their foreign exchange earnings to the central bank, even though they may be offered a higher price elsewhere. The controls may require that importers of goods, services and securities buy foreign exchange from the central bank, which may sell only limited amounts at the parity rates; importers may be limited in their purchases of foreign exchange to amounts acquired in previous periods. Importers of specified goods and securities may be obliged to pay a higher price for foreign exchange than importers of other goods; the country then follows multiple exchange rate practices.

Exchange controls cause the effective price of foreign exchange to differ from the parity rate. In effect, changes in these controls are an indirect way to change the exchange rate.[3] Such controls almost always lead to the development of a black or illegal market in foreign exchange, since some traders and investors find it in their interests to evade the controls. The spread between the black market rate and the parity becomes one indicator of the severity of controls.

While exchange controls have traditionally been used by countries with weak currencies to maintain overvalued parities, countries with strong currencies also have used these controls to alter their payments balances. Initially, the countries with large payments surpluses may reduce their controls over access to foreign exchange by domestic residents as a way to reduce these surpluses. After such controls have been eliminated, they may limit the ability of foreign residents to acquire domestic securities; domestic banks may be prohibited from paying interest on foreign-owned deposits and foreigners may be restricted from buying domestic securities. Both Germany and Switzerland have adopted a variety of such measures to limit foreign purchases of mark and Swiss franc assets.

The more frequently a country changes its exchange parity, the more nearly a pegged rate system approaches a floating rate system. Brazil and Colombia have a 'crawling peg'; the parity is changed every four or five weeks by 2 or 3 per cent. Thus far, the monetary authorities have used discretion in deciding the frequency and the amount of the changes in the pegs; they recognise that they may have to alter their parities by 20 or 25 per cent over the course of a year, and they determine the number of mini-devaluations required so that no one change will be so large as to be disruptive. Such changes might be keyed to a formula which would rely on changes in the central bank holdings of international monies as a trigger for changing the peg.

Several factors stand out in appraising developments in exchange market arrangements in the last twenty years. After an extended period in which most changes in parities involved devaluations, the currencies of many European countries and Japan were revalued in 1971. Moreover, parity changes became increasingly frequent. Subsequently, many countries permitted their currencies to float in 1973. These several factors reflect the impact of national monetary policies and divergent inflation rates in causing the established structure of parity rates to become obsolete.

NATIONAL MONETARY POLICIES AND THE EXCHANGE RATE

The monetary policies followed in different countries can be grouped by the targets followed by their central bank authorities in determining the rates at which their national money supplies will grow. Some countries have pursued dependent monetary policies; changes in their domestic money supplies are geared to changes in their central banks' holdings of international monies – primarily gold and dollars.[4] The key feature of a dependent monetary policy is that changes in the central bank's holdings of international money produce automatic changes in its domestic money supply in a more or less mechanical fashion. The domestic money supply increases when the central bank purchases foreign exchange from exporters by issuing more domestic monetary liabilities; its domestic monetary liabilities decline when importers buy foreign exchange and pay with domestic money. The domestic monetary liabilities of the central bank are constant as long as its holdings of international money are constant.

Assume Ruthenia is initially in balance-of-payments equilibrium; the payments of domestic residents to non-residents for purchases of goods equal its export receipts from foreigners, so that its central bank's holdings of international money are constant. Then the foreign demand for Ruthenian goods increases. Ruthenia develops a payments surplus; its central bank buys dollars from exporters. The Ruthenian money supply increases. In contrast, had Ruthenia developed a payments deficit, perhaps because the foreign demand for its exports had declined, its central bank would have sold dollars to importers and its domestic money supply would have decreased.

Payments imbalances – both deficits and surpluses – tend to be self-correcting with dependent monetary policies. As the Ruthenian money supply falls as a result of its payments deficit, Ruthenians demand fewer domestic goods. Ruthenian prices fall, and Ruthenian goods become increasingly price-competitive with foreign goods, both in Ruthenia and in various foreign markets. Ruthenian exports increase, its imports decline and its payments deficit becomes smaller. As long as the payments deficit continues, even at the diminishing level, the Ruthenian money supply declines, and domestic prices decline, albeit at a slower rate. Eventually, Ruthenian prices fall to the level at which a payments balance is attained; then, its money supply remains constant until another disturbance occurs. The decline in Ruthenian price level means that Ruthenia can continue to maintain its exchange parity.

Similarly, as long as Ruthenia follows a dependent monetary policy, it is automatically protected from the need to revalue its currency as a result of a large payments surplus. The increase in the domestic money supply caused by a payments surplus leads to increases in Ruthenian prices; Ruthenian goods become less competitive in international markets. Exports from Ruthenia decline while imports increase. The increase in Ruthenian prices relative to world prices leads to a diminishing payments surplus. As long as the payments surplus continues, however, the Ruthenian money supply increases and domestic prices increase. Eventually, Ruthenian prices increase to the level at which a payments balance is attained.

Consequently, as long as countries follow dependent monetary policies and permit their price levels to be determined by changes in their holdings of international money, the need to change their parities should not arise. Parity changes mean that central banks do not follow dependent monetary policies, because they are unwilling to accept the resulting variations in levels of prices and employment associated with such policies.

An independent monetary policy means that the central bank focuses on one or several domestic objectives – the employment level, the price level, the rate of economic growth, the level of government expenditures – in determining the rate of domestic monetary expansion. The impact of changes in the volume of monetary liabilities on the country's payments position and its holdings of international money is not given high priority. Yet variations in the rate of domestic monetary expansion affect the country's balance of payments and its holdings of international money by their impact on domestic prices, incomes, interest rates, and on the volume of trade in goods and in securities. Changes in domestic prices and incomes affect the demand for foreign goods and securities, and the supplies of domestic goods and securities available for export. Increases in domestic prices lead to a reduction in international competitiveness, so that imports increase relative to exports; similarly, increases in domestic incomes also lead to increases in imports relative to exports of goods.

The payments deficits and surpluses incurred by a country that follows an independent monetary policy are not self-correcting, as they are with a dependent monetary policy. While the payments deficit and the reduction in the central bank's holding of international money mean that the domestic money supply should fall, the monetary authority purchases additional domestic monetary assets to forestall any decline in the domestic money supply. As long as countries follow independent monetary policies, changes in exchange rates are necessary to restore payments equilibrium.

Countries on the gold standard in the years prior to the First World War followed dependent monetary policies. During the last fifty years, countries have increasingly oriented their monetary policies towards their domestic objectives; more and more have followed independent monetary policies.[5] A consequence is that national price levels have increased at somewhat different rates. Eventually the countries with the more rapidly rising prices have found it necessary to devalue their currencies or to permit their currencies to float – and to depreciate.

CHANGES IN THE SUPPLY OF INTERNATIONAL MONEY AS A SHOCK TO EXCHANGE RATES

Variations in the rate of growth of international money may have an inflationary or deflationary impact on national economies and hence on the alignment of exchange rates. If the supply of international money grows rapidly, many countries may simultaneously have payments surpluses, and their domestic money supplies are likely to grow rapidly. New gold discoveries in North America and South Africa at the end of the nineteenth century led to increases in money supplies in various countries and imparted an upward thrust to the commodity price levels in many countries, although not necessarily at the same rate. One consequence of the rapid growth in the supply of international money is that many countries may 'import inflation' at the same time. These countries then face the choice between accepting the more rapid-than-desired increases in their domestic price levels, or revaluing their currencies or permitting them to appreciate. Conversely, a shortage of international money may have a deflationary impact, and some countries might devalue their currencies to increase their holdings of international money – as many did in the early 1930s.

Assets become international money in response to the search for monetary stability. Thus gold became a monetary asset because of the confidence in the stability of its value in terms of a wide range of other commodities. Changes in the gold holdings of central banks reflect the difference between the cumulative amount of gold produced and the cumulative amount demanded for private uses. The increase in monetary gold holdings in the 1930s resulted from the sharp increase in the monetary price of gold relative to the costs of gold production, while the diminution in the rate of increase in monetary gold holdings in the 1950s and 1960s resulted from the combination of a fixed monetary price and increases in costs of production as commodity price levels rose.

Central banks began to hold liquid assets denominated in dollars, sterling and other national currencies as international money because such assets appeared likely to remain stable in value and, unlike gold, offered interest income. The volume of this component of international reserves increased modestly until the late 1960s. One consequence of the combination of the U.S. inflation and the rigidity of the exchange rate structure of the late 1960s was that the United States incurred an increasingly large payments deficit, whose mirror was the increasingly large surpluses in Western Europe and Japan. The persistence of the payments imbalance, because of the reluctance of both the surplus countries and the United States to take the initiative in changing parities, meant that the dollar component of international money increased sharply. Eventually, dissatisfaction with the inflationary consequences of large increases in international money holdings led to changes in exchange rates.

The growth of the international moneys issued by the International Monetary Fund, both in the form of Reserve Positions in the Fund and Special Drawing Rights (SDRs), resulted from the demand for fiat money not tied to one country's currency. The supply of IMF-produced international monies is determined by negotiations among its members; thus far this component of the total supply of international money has been small and not a disturbance to the exchange rate structure.

STRUCTURAL CHANGE AS A SHOCK TO THE EXCHANGE RATES

Most of the changes in exchange rates observed in the post-war period can be attributed to monetary phenomena, either to variations in growth of domestic monies, or to variations in the rate of growth of international monies. Some changes in parities, however, have non-monetary sources, in that the currencies of some countries appreciate even though their price levels are increasing more rapidly than those of their trading partners. The inclusive, generic term for non-monetary disturbances is structural change. Some countries may discover new mineral resources; their exports may increase even while their domestic price levels remain unchanged relative to the world price levels. Thus Venezuela revalued the bolivar after the sharp increase in the world price of petroleum.[6] Rapid gains in productivity in exports or tradeable goods industries – and hence a decline in the export prices of these goods – may lead to an increase in exports even though the more comprehensive wholesale or consumer price levels are stable or increasing. The payments surpluses may lead to an increase in the money supplies and perhaps to higher domestic prices. Export-oriented industries grew very rapidly in Japan in the 1960s, and the Japanese balance-of-payments position improved, even though consumer prices in Japan were rising more rapidly than in its major trading partners. Germany regained its position as a major world supplier of machinery after much of its industry had been destroyed in the Second World War, and its export earnings increased sharply.

Changes in exchange rates are used to restore balance in international payments in response to structural disturbances; the alternative – as with dependent monetary policies – involves changes in the domestic price level. Japan revalued in 1971; Germany in 1961, 1969 and 1971.

Because changes in economic structure occur continuously, it might seem that many exchange rate changes could be attributed to structural factors. Structural changes usually occur gradually; the increase in the world price of petroleum is an exception. The frequency of changes in exchange rates attributable to structural disturbances is an empirical issue and is discussed in Chapter 5.

MONETARY SYSTEMS AND THE PATTERN OF EXCHANGE RATE CHANGES

Each system consists of a set of national monetary policies, exchange market arrangements and international monies. The textbook gold standard was one system; each country followed a dependent monetary policy, the parities for national currencies were stated in terms of gold and gold was used as international money. Changes in exchange rates were virtually impossible as long as variations in the domestic money supplies resulted only from payments surpluses and deficits, and exchange rates remained pegged except in response to major political events like wars and revolutions. Variations in national price levels reflected changes in the supply of international money and were accepted to maintain the gold parities.

The gold standard was gradually abandoned because countries wanted greater control over their economic destinies – over their price and employment levels. Inevitably, the shift towards independent monetary policies meant that changes in exchange rates would be more frequent.

The monetary arrangement during the 1946–71 period was based on the Articles of Agreement of the International Monetary Fund and known as the Bretton Woods system. Member countries could follow either dependent or independent monetary policies; each was required to state a parity for its currency. Floating exchange rates were proscribed. Most parities were stated in terms of the U.S. dollar, while the parity for the dollar was expressed in terms of gold. Exchange market support limits were limited to 1 per cent either side of parity.

Fund's Articles of Agreement stipulated that a member country could change its parity only if it were in 'fundamental disequilibrium'. While this term was not defined operationally, the meaning was clear – the existing parity was not one at which the country could achieve a satisfactory payments balance, except with undesirably high levels of unemployment or of exchange controls. A member country might change its parity without the Fund's approval if the proposed change was no more than 10 per cent from its original parity. If the proposed change were larger, the Fund might delay the change, and it might disapprove. In the absence of Fund approval, the member might change its parity, subject to possible sanctions from the Fund or from other member countries.

Under the IMF system, most member countries supported their currencies in the exchange market by buying and selling dollars; the dollar was their intervention currency. As long as other countries pegged their currencies to the dollar it was unnecessary for the U.S. authorities to support the dollar in the exchange market.[7] Foreign central banks used the dollar as the intervention currency because a large part of their foreign exchange transactions involved the dollar.

Since the Fund began operations, member countries changed their parities more than one hundred times. Most members changed their parities in accordance with Fund rules. Before 1970 only Canada and Lebanon had used floating rates for an extended period – Canada from 1950 to 1962 and Lebanon after 1950. More than twenty members, however, had adopted floating rates as an interim measure pending a move from one parity to another. From 1970 onwards, however, the Fund rules were violated with greater frequency and by larger countries, and the credibility of the rules declined.

The components of the Bretton Woods system were not fully consistent. Thus one institutional feature of the gold standard, the parity, was retained even though independent monetary policies and larger differences in national rates of inflation meant that changes in exchange rates were inevitable.

The succession of international financial crises in the late 1960s and early 1970s resulted from the inconsistency among central bank monetary policies, the exchange rate system, and the supply of international monies. Central banks followed increasingly independent monetary policies; full employment and rapid growth were deemed more important than stability in their price levels or balance-of-payments equilibrium. National central banks wanted to retain their parities, even as their payments imbalances increased. The governments in countries with persistent payments deficits were reluctant to devalue – some believed that devaluations would increase domestic inflation, others viewed such changes as a failure of their economic policies. The governments in countries with payments surpluses were reluctant to revalue, since profits and employment in industries producing exports and import-competing goods would be adversely affected. As a result of the delays in changing parities, the disequilibria in international payments became large.

Economic factors set the necessary preconditions for devaluations and revaluations. The decisions to alter parities, and to cease (or begin) pegging currencies, are political because of their impacts on the distribution of income, employment, price levels and the returns in the next elections.[8] Necessary changes in exchange rates are delayed because the immediate political costs seem higher than the gains; in a period of full employment, the costs of delaying a change in a parity that might prove necessary seem lower than the costs of effecting a change that might otherwise prove unnecessary.

Anticipation of the forthcoming changes in parities led investors to shift funds to avoid losses from such changes – and to profit from them. As the imbalance persisted, investors became increasingly confident that the parity would be changed while the authorities debated whether to change the rate and by how much. Frequently investors were right. Occasionally they were wrong, by anticipating changes that did not occur, as with sterling prior to 1967, and as with the Italian lira in 1963. Under the pre-1971 arrangements, the costs to investors of being wrong were small compared with the gains of being right. Increasingly, the expectations that parities would be changed proved correct, and speculative pressure against currencies in the early 1970s was much more intense than earlier.

For much of the post-war period, changes in the exchange parities of individual countries were not correlated with each other. The revaluations in 1971, and the shift to floating exchange rates in 1973, affected the currencies of most industrial countries simultaneously.

The revaluations reflected the shortcomings in the arrangements for supplying the demand for international money. In the 1950s and 1960s most of the newly produced gold was absorbed into private uses, since private parties were willing to pay a higher price for gold than central banks were. Gold was under-priced – the amount demanded by central banks at $35 exceeded the supply available from new production, and as a result central banks could only buy gold from each other.

The U.S. payments deficit during the 1950s and much of the 1960s reflected that the demand for international money exceeded the supply available from non-U.S. sources. The United States produced international money in the form of dollar-denominated liabilities; in addition, the U.S. Treasury was a large seller of gold and U.S. holdings declined from 1949 to1971. Until 1966 or 1967 the United States sold gold and dollars to foreign central banks, not because the dollar was overvalued, but rather because various countries wanted to add to their holdings of gold and dollar-denominated assets. Few countries appeared to have undervalued currencies – with the exception of Germany. The U.S. international reserve position became weaker, while the positions of most other industrial countries became stronger. The paradox was that the acquisition of dollar assets by foreign central banks because the dollar appeared strong eventually caused the dollar to appear weaker.

After 1968, the U.S. payments deficit became larger than might be explained in terms of the demand of foreign central banks for international money. The U.S. inflation associated with the Vietnam war caused a surge in the U.S. payments deficit; U.S. imports increased sharply. Some foreign central banks acquired more dollars than they wished, and believed they were importing the U.S. inflation.

Then the policy issue was whether the United States should devalue the dollar or the surplus countries, e.g. Canada, Japan, Germany, France and others, should revalue their currencies. Economically, the difference between revaluations of those currencies by 10 per cent or a devaluation of the dollar by 10 per cent was small. But there was substantial difference in political terms. The United States wanted the surplus countries to revalue so that the $35 parity might be retained; they felt the United States should devalue because the large imbalance was triggered by the U.S. inflation.

In August 1971 the U.S. authorities formally suspended gold sales at the $35 parity. At the same time the United States also levied a 10 per cent import surcharge as a back-door way to induce foreign countries to revalue their currencies; the premise was that the surcharge would be removed after they revalued. A number of industrial countries, including Great Britain, Italy, Japan and Switzerland, allowed their currencies to float; indeed for the last four months of 1971 the currencies of all the industrial countries floated.

At the end of 1971 a new set of pegged exchange rates was formalised in the Smithsonian Agreement. Twelve currencies were revalued relative to the U.S. dollar, on average by about 10 per cent, and the import surcharge was withdrawn. The Canadian dollar continued to float. Support limits were modestly widened. In June 1972 speculation against sterling led the British to permit sterling to float again. Several months later, speculators believed that a revaluation of the yen was inevitable –

and imminent – and greatly increased their demand for yen assets.

In February 1973 a second dollar-centred crisis erupted; the exchange rate structure negotiated in the Smithsonian Agreement came unstuck, and with it investor confidence in the ability of the authorities to manage a pegged rate system. The major currencies began to float. For a pegged rate system is viable only if changes in exchange rates are relatively infrequent, and market participants have credibility in the continuity of the parities.

The mark and other European currencies appreciated, and for a while quite sharply relative to the dollar. One contributing factor was the contractive German monetary policy; investors responded to the increase in mark interest rates with a substantial increase in the demand for mark assets.

The currencies of Belgium, the Netherlands, Switzerland and other continental European currencies moved with the mark. The member countries of the European Community had planned to move to a unified monetary policy much as they had a uniform tariff and a uniform agricultural policy. They intervened in the exchange market so that their currencies would appreciate and depreciate at about the same rate. The joint float, known as the 'snake in the tunnel' arrangement, required substantial consultation on their intervention practices. On several occasions the mark was revalued relative to the other currencies in the snake. Italy and then France dropped out of the arrangement; France rejoined in mid-1975 and left in early 1976. Nevertheless, an informal mark area began to develop; the movements of exchange rates between the mark and the other European currencies were substantially smaller than between these currencies and the dollar. Even though the Swiss did not participate formally in the joint float, the Swiss franc moved sympathetically with the mark, for much of Swiss trade is with Germany and other nearby countries.

In the late summer of 1973 the dollar appeared cheap. Then the fourfold increase in the price of crude petroleum led investors to sell the European currencies, and they depreciated. By the end of 1973 the exchange rates against the dollar were roughly those of a year earlier, when the currencies began to float.

In late 1974 and early 1975 interest rates on dollar assets fell sharply. Moreover, reports indicated that oil-producing countries were seeking to diversify their reserve assets, and hold a larger share of their wealth in assets denominated in various European currencies. As a consequence, the European currencies appreciated, almost as sharply as in the spring of 1973.

In mid-1977 the price of the dollar in terms of the mark, the guilder and the currencies of several other European currencies was about the same as in early 1973, when most currencies began to float. In the intervening four-year period the price of the dollar had moved within a range of 15–20 per cent.

These movements in exchange rates were much sharper than changes in relative price levels. Frequently the central banks in most of the countries intervened in the exchange market, both to limit sudden sharp movements in the rate and to prevent their currencies from becoming either excessively undervalued or excessively overvalued. Intervention was on an *ad hoc* basis.[9]

REFORM OF THE SYSTEM

For a decade there has been considerable debate about the need for a new international financial system, one which would be less subject to crises. A new system would contain treaty-based rules directed at central bank behaviour in the exchange market; in the absence of rules there is the risk that countries might again follow 'beggar thy neighbour' policies as in the 1930s, and seek to export unemployment or inflation. The new rules would involve a set of commitments about central bank operations in the exchange market, and would specify when intervention is permissible, when it is obligatory, and when it is unacceptable.

Some countries, including France and many smaller countries, favour a return to a pegged rate system. A return to pegged rates is not feasible as long as rates of inflation differ significantly among major countries. As long as inflation rates are as high as 5 or 6 per cent a year, a pegged rate system on the Bretton Woods model is not feasible. A new system must necessarily provide for much more frequent changes in parities, and contain wider support limits. Hence the differences between the feasible set of pegged rates and a system of managed floating rates would be somewhat smaller.

Even when relative price stability is attained, the return to a pegged exchange rate regime would not lead to a crisis-free arrangement. One approach to such an arrangement would involve harmonisation of national monetary policies; ultimately, this approach involves unification of national currencies. Most countries appear unlikely to give up the advantages they associate with a national money. The effective harmonisation of monetary policy across a broad range of countries seems unlikely.

An alternative approach to reform involves developing a framework that would permit countries to follow independent monetary policies and yet reduce the trauma associated with the inevitable changes in exchange rates. Thus there are a variety of proposals for greater flexibility in the exchange parities, either on a discretionary or a formula basis. Since the crises are associated with a build-up of speculative pressure for a change in the parity, the idea common to these proposals is that the speculative pressure will be smaller if the exchange rate is changed more frequently and hence by a smaller amount. But some countries appear reluctant to adopt this approach, because they fear they would lose control over their exchange rates; the exchange rates might be determined by short-term capital flows or other transient phenomena.

As long as countries follow independent monetary policies, changes in exchange rates will occur. What is uncertain is the arrangement for changing the rates – how much of the adjustment will involve changes in exchange rates and whether currencies will be pegged or float.

SUMMARY

Changes in exchange rates reflect the desires of individual countries to pursue monetary policies appropriate to their domestic economic objectives. Through most of the post-war period the devaluations were a result of more rapid increases in prices abroad than in the United States. However, the revaluations of 1971 and 1973 reflect the more rapid U.S. inflation. The shift to floating rates reflects the erosion of the commitment to pegged rates, and the inability of the central bankers to set a new value for parities in which investors would have confidence.

3. Exchange Risk and Yield Differentials

Changes in exchange rates are inevitable in a world of more than one hundred national currencies. Investors may be able to advance their economic welfare by acquiring assets denominated in currencies they expect to appreciate and selling assets and issuing liabilities denominated in currencies they expect to depreciate. As investors revise their holdings of assets denominated in different currencies, exchange rates should change. At any moment individual investors must determine whether the anticipated changes in the exchange rates have been fully discounted in other economic variables, or whether there remains an unexploited profit opportunity.

This chapter focuses on several proportionality propositions which link both commodity price levels in several countries and interest rates on assets denominated in various currencies with changes in exchange rates; these propositions are variants on the theme that the price levels, interest rates and exchange rates fully adjust to changes in the money supply—money demand relationship.

THE LAW OF ONE PRICE

The Law of One Price is a proposition about the relationships among the prices of identical assets and commodities in different geographic centres. The simplest form of the Law states that identical assets must sell at the same price at the same time in the same market. The Law reflects the response of rational investors to unexploited profit opportunities. Arbitragers buy the asset in the centre where it is cheap and sell it in the centre where it is expensive as long as the price differential exceeds transport and transactions costs. The price differential between a given quantity of wheat in Kansas City and in Chicago can be no greater than transport costs:

$$\left| P_w^{KC} - P_w^C \right| \leq T$$

where P_w^{KC} is the price of wheat in Kansas City, P_w^C the price in Chicago, and T transport costs per unit of wheat. The superscripts refer to the centres in which the wheat is traded, and the subscripts identify the commodity. The higher the transport costs, the larger the possible spread between the prices in the two centres. Tariffs, quotas and other barriers to the shipment of commodities and other assets among countries, as well as barriers to the shipment of money, may explain persistent price differentials in excess of transport costs.

The prices of the same financial asset in two countries can be compared only if they are expressed in one currency; then, the difference in prices should conform to the Law of One Price, provided that both the asset and money can be freely imported and exported. The franc price of IBM shares in Paris cannot differ significantly from the New York dollar price, as long as the transport costs and the transactions costs are negligible. Thus,

$$\left| P_{IBM}^{NY} - \left(P_{IBM}^{P} \cdot \frac{1}{F/\$} \right) \right| \leqq T$$

where $1/F/\$)$ is the exchange rate.

Provided transport costs are low and national barriers to the movement of the assets are not substantial, transactions in various countries occur in the same worldwide market in that price movements in one centre are reflected in similar price movements elsewhere. The stock exchanges in New York, London, Paris, Zürich and Amsterdam are sections of one world market; the shares of many large companies are traded on the exchanges in several countries. The larger the transactions costs and the higher the national barriers to the movement of assets, the greater the maximum differential between the price of an asset in one centre and its price in other countries.

The Law of One Price can be extended to the price relationship among similar, non-identical assets in the same centre. The price spread between two similar assets can be no greater than the costs incurred in converting the low-price asset into the high-price asset. Thus,

$$\left| P_x^A - P_{x'}^A \right| \leq C$$

where x is one commodity, x' a similar, non-identical commodity, and C the conversion cost per unit of x. The price spread may be less than C, for consumers of the higher-price asset will be attracted to the lower-price asset as the price differential increases relative to the quality differential.

If assets are identical and transactions costs minimal, lags between changes in the price of the asset in the one centre and price changes elsewhere may be small and unobservable. The less identical the assets and the higher the transactions costs, the longer the possible delay between the changes in the price in one centre and similar price changes elsewhere.

The Law of One Price has a temporal extension which relates the spot price of commodities or assets with the prices of future contracts for these commodities or assets. The statement is

$$\left| P_C^F - P_C^S \right| \leq S$$

where P_C^F is the price of copper futures contracts, P_C^S the spot price, and S the storage costs, which includes both the interest cost on the funds invested in the commodity and the expense incurred in storing the commodity. The explanation is that as the price of futures contracts rises relative to the spot price, arbitragers buy the commodity spot and sell futures contracts; on the maturity of the futures contract, they might deliver the commodity to those who hold the long position in the futures contract.

The prospect of large harvests might be expected to lead to a sharp decline in spot price in the future. Those who own the product sell from their inventories to minimise their losses, and so the spot price should decline immediately in anticipation of the declines in the future; such sales are likely to continue as long as the commodity is held in inventories.

THE PURCHASING POWER PARITY THEORY

The Purchasing Power Parity Theory is a statement about the commodity price level in one country, the world commodity price level, and the equilibrium exchange rate for the country's currency – that rate at which the country is in payments equilibrium. The absolute version of the theory states that the equilibrium exchange rate is the ratio of the price of a representative market basket of domestic goods to the price of an identical market basket of world goods. Thus if the same commodities are included in the same proportions in the domestic market basket and the world basket, the absolute version must necessarily be valid; Purchasing Power Parity is the same as the Law of One Price with an identical composite commodity. Whereas the Law of One Price deals with individual commodities, Purchasing Power Parity involves bundles of commodities, including non-traded goods and services as well as goods and services which are traded internationally. Deviations from the absolute version of Purchasing Power Parity can occur only if transactions costs or barriers to the movement of goods internationally are significant, or if the market basket of domestic goods differs in content or proportions from the world market basket.

The relative version of Purchasing Power Parity states that the rate of change in the equilibrium exchange rate is proportional to the difference between the rates of change in the domestic price level and the world price level. The relative version is less restrictive than the absolute version; the relative version may be valid even if the absolute version is not. In the absolute version, the statement is

$$e = \frac{P_d}{P_f}$$

where e is the exchange rate expressed as the number of D's currency units required to buy 1 unit of F's currency, P_f the commodity price level in country F, and P_d the domestic commodity price level. In the relative version, the statement is

$$\frac{\dot{e}}{e} = \frac{\dot{P}_d}{P_d} - \frac{\dot{P}_f}{P_f}$$

where the dots refer to rate of change.

Fig. 3.1 illustrates the relative version of Purchasing Power Parity.[1] The difference between the rates of change in the domestic price level and the world price level is measured on the horizontal axis; the rate of change in the exchange rate is measured on the vertical axis.[2] The *PPP* function is represented by a line which intersects the two axes at a 45° angle. Each value for the difference between the rates of change in the two price levels, such as P^1 and P^2, implies a unique rate of change in the equilibrium exchange rate, such as E^1 and E^2. As the domestic

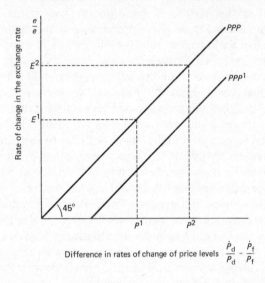

Fig. 3.1.
The Purchasing Power Parity Theory (in rates of changes).

price level rises relative to the world price level at the rate P^1, domestic currency depreciates at the rate E^1; the more rapid the increase in the domestic price level, the more rapid the depreciation of domestic currency.

Purchasing Power Parity Theory implies causality — that changes in the price level relationship induce changes in the exchange rate. The statement that the equilibrium exchange rate must change if the price level relationship changes does not mean that the equilibrium exchange rate may not change when relative price levels remain unchanged. At issue is whether there can be meaningful deviations from the relative version of Purchasing Power Parity, in either the short run or the long run, which might be attributed to structural factors, such as the discovery of petroleum, changes in the demand for imports, or changes in the rate of foreign investment. In these examples, the demand of foreign residents for domestic currency might change even if the relationship between domestic prices and world prices is not unchanged.[3] These structural changes are shown by a rightward shift of the *PPP* function in Fig. 3.1 to *PPP*[1], which continues as long as the structural change causes a movement in the equilibrium exchange rate;[4] this shift is independent of changes in relative prices.

The actual exchange rate may deviate from the equilibrium rate, both with floating exchange rates and with pegged exchange rates. The extent of the deviations between the actual rate and the equilibrium exchange rate depends on a variety of factors, including the size of the foreign trade sector relative to the economy, differences among countries in rates of productivity gain in the non-traded goods industries and the traded goods industries, and changes in exchange controls. The smaller the foreign trade sector, the less representative changes in the price level ratio may be of changes in the country's international competitive position. The larger the differences between productivity gains in non-traded goods industries and in traded goods industries, the more likely the actual exchange rate will differ from the equilibrium rate predicted from changes in price level ratios. The greater the changes in exchange controls and in other barriers to international payments, the greater the possible deviation from Purchasing Power Parity.

Observed changes in exchange rates may confirm or deny Purchasing Power Parity, depending on whether the source of the payments disequilibrium is monetary or structural. The German revaluations in 1969 and 1971 reflected both monetary and structural factors. The German price level had risen modestly less rapidly than the price levels of its trading partners and so revaluations of the mark would have been necessary to adjust for this difference. But a revaluation probably would have been necessary even if the relationship between price levels was unchanged, for world tastes were shifting towards the types of goods in which Germany was a low-cost producer. Similarly, the Japanese revaluation in 1971 had a structural cause; while Japanese prices on average had risen more rapidly than those in its major trading partners, the prices of Japanese finished manufactures – steel, cars, electronics – had fallen. Japanese goods had become more competitive internationally; Japan's export earnings increased sharply. Whether observed changes in exchange rates in the last twenty five years can be better explained by monetary or structural causes is considered in Chapter 5.

THE FISHER EFFECTS: FISHER CLOSED AND FISHER OPEN

Two proportionality propositions involve money interest rates and changes in commodity price levels.[5] The Fisher Closed proposition is that the money (or nominal) rate of interest reflects the anticipated real rate of interest and the anticipated rate of change in the commodity price level. Thus, $r_m = r_r^* + \dot{\pi}^*$, where r_m is the money interest rate, r_r^* the anticipated real rate of interest and $\dot{\pi}^*$ the anticipated rate of change in the commodity price level; the asterisks indicate anticipated values. If investors anticipate that the commodity price level will not change, the money rate of interest will be identical with the anticipated real rate of interest. If investors anticipate that the commodity price level will increase at the rate of 5 per cent a year, the money rate of interest should exceed the anticipated real rate of interest by 5 percentage points on an annualised basis for all maturities of securities. If investors anticipate that the commodity price level will increase at a more rapid rate in the distant future than in the near future, then the interest rates on longer-term securities should exceed those on securities with shorter maturities. That money interest rates change as the anticipations about the future price level change reflects that investors borrow to finance acquisition of

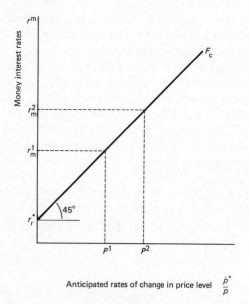

Fig. 3.2.
The Fisher effect in the closed economy.

commodities as long as the anticipated inventory profits exceed the borrowing costs. Similarly, investors will acquire and hold monetary assets only if the money interest rates are sufficiently high to compensate for the anticipated increases in the commodity price level.

Fisher Closed is illustrated in Fig. 3.2. The anticipated rate of change in the commodity price level, $(p/p)^*$ is measured on the horizontal axis, while both the anticipated real rate of interest, r_r^*, and the money interest rate, r_m, are measured on the vertical axis. The F_c locus shows the money interest rate associated with each anticipated rate of change in the commodity price level; this locus intersects the vertical axis at a 45° angle, at the level of the anticipated real rate of interest. If investors anticipate that the commodity price level will not change, the money and real rates of interest should be the same. When P^1 is the anticipated rate of change of the price level, r_m^1 is the money interest rate; when P^2 is the anticipated rate of change, then r_m^2 is the money interest rate. The higher the anticipated rate of increase in the commodity price level, the higher the money rate of interest. A reduction in the anticipated real rate of interest leads to a rightward shift in the F_c locus.

Differences between the observed money interest rate and the rates inferred from changes in the commodity price level indicate that investor foresight is imperfect; in some periods the increases in the price level may exceed the money interest rate and at other periods the reverse may be true. Systematic differences between observed interest rates and real interest rates larger or smaller than the rates of change in the commodity level suggest an inefficiency in the capital market, in that investors appear not to exploit fully an apparent profit opportunity.

The Fisher Open proposition is that the differences in money interest rates on similar assets denominated in several currencies equal the anticipated rates of change in the exchange rate. Thus, $r_d - r_f = (\dot{e}/e)^*$, where $(\dot{e}/e)^*$ is the anticipated rate of change in the exchange rate, r_d the domestic money interest rate, and r_f the foreign (or world) money interest rate. If investors anticipate that the price of foreign exchange will increase at a constant rate of 2 per cent a year, domestic interest rates should exceed foreign interest rates by 2 percentage points for all maturities of securities. If investors anticipate that the price of foreign exchange will increase more rapidly in the distant future, then the interest rate differential (hereafter the interest agio) should be larger on securities with distant maturities than on those with near maturities.

The rationale for Fisher Open is that investors hold assets denominated in currencies expected to depreciate only if the interest rates on these assets are sufficiently high to compensate for the capital loss from the anticipated change in the exchange rate. Similarly, investors hold assets denominated in currencies which they anticipate will appreciate at lower interest rates because of the prospective capital gain from the changes in the exchange rate.

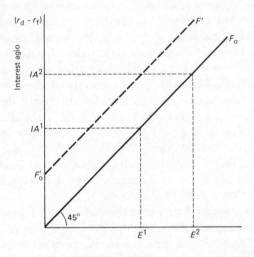

Fig. 3.3.
The Fisher effect in an open economy.

Fig. 3.3 illustrates Fisher Open in a two-currency world. The anticipated rate of change in the exchange rate, $\dot{e}^*$, is measured on the horizontal axis, and the interest agio, $r_d - r_f$, for any pair of securities with identical maturities, is measured on the vertical axis. Fisher Open (F_0) is represented by a line which intersects the two axes at a 45 angle. For each anticipated rate of change in the exchange rate, such as E^1 and E^2, there is a unique equilibrium interest agio, such as IA^1 and IA^2. The higher the anticipated rate of change in the exchange rate, the larger the interest agio. If investors have a modest preference for assets denominated in one currency (perhaps because of tax considerations) after recognition of the anticipated change in the exchange rate, the F_0 function intersects the vertical axis at some point other than the horizontal axis, such as F'_0.

Assume investors anticipate that the pengo will depreciate at a rate of 10 per cent a year, perhaps because the Ruthenian price level is increasing at 10 per cent a year when the world price level is unchanged. If interest rates on pengo-denominated bonds are less than 10 percentage points higher than those on dollar bonds, investors would sell pengo bonds and buy dollar bonds. The price of pengo bonds would decline; their interest rates would increase. Perhaps, investor purchases of dollar bonds would lead to increases in their price, although most of the adjustment in interest rates will involve those of the smaller country. Thus the interest agio adjusts to the anticipated rate of change in the exchange rate.[6]

This discussion of Fisher Open has proceeded as if investors operate in a certain world and adjust their demands for securities denominated in the several currencies on the basis of anticipated changes in exchange rates. Whether Fisher Open holds in an uncertain world is an empirical issue. Some of the anticipated changes in exchange rates may occur; some may not. The rates of monetary expansion are affected by political factors, and so a view about prospective changes in exchange rates requires views on monetary policies in the future in the several countries. Deviations between the predicted exchange rates for various dates inferred from the interest agios and the observed exchange rates on these dates result from imperfections in investor foresight. The empirical question is whether these deviations are random or systematic, and if systematic, why investors have not exploited the profit opportunity.

THE INTEREST RATE PARITY THEOREM

The Interest Rate Parity Theorem relates the exchange rates on forward contracts of specified maturities to the money market interest agios on similar assets denominated in different currencies. The forward exchange rate is the price on a contract to exchange bank deposits denominated in different currencies at a specified future date. Whereas spot exchange contracts involve commitments to exchange deposits two days after the date when the parties agree to the contract, forward contracts involve commitments to exchange deposits at more distant dates. Common maturities are one month, three months and six months; other maturities are also available.[7]

The forward exchange rate is a free price set by market forces. IMF member countries were not obliged to maintain the forward exchange rate within their support limits. Central banks occasionally have intervened in the forward market, both to influence flows of interest-sensitive funds and to forestall speculative pressure.

The absolute difference between the spot exchange rate and the forward exchange rate is readily converted to an annual percentage differential (hereafter the exchange agio); thus,

$$X = A\left(\frac{F-S}{S}\right)$$

where X is the exchange agio in percentage terms on an annual basis, A is a factor to convert the absolute difference in the two exchange rates to an annualised value, F is the forward exchange rate, and S the spot exchange rate. The values of A vary with the maturity of the forward contract; A has the value of 1.00 on one-year forward contracts and 4.00 on three-month contracts. If the spot exchange rate is 4 pengos equal $1.00 and the exchange rate on forward contracts of one-month maturity is 4.02 pengos equal $1.00, then the exchange agio is

$$12.00\left(\frac{4.02-4.00}{4.00}\right) = 6 \text{ per cent}$$

The pengo is at a forward discount, since it is less expensive in the forward market than in the spot market.

The Interest Rate Parity Theorem states that the exchange agio equals the interest agio for each maturity date; the expression is[8]

$$A\left(\frac{F-S}{S}\right) = \frac{r_d - r_f}{1 + r_f}, \quad \begin{array}{l} \text{where } r_d \text{ is the pengo interest rate and } r_f \\ \text{the dollar interest rate.} \end{array}$$

If the Interest Rate Parity Theorem is valid, then in the previous example interest rates on pengo-denominated money market assets would be 6 percentage points higher than on similar dollar-denominated assets.[9] Fig. 3.4 illustrates the Interest Rate Parity Theorem. The interest agio is measured on the horizontal axis; domestic interest rates are higher than foreign interest rates to the right of the origin. The exchange agio is measured on the vertical axis; domestic currency is at a forward discount above the origin.[10] The 45° line indicates the predicted relationship between the spot and the forward exchange rates for each value of the interest agio.

The rationale for the Interest Rate Parity Theorem is identical with

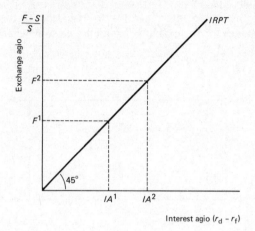

Fig. 3.4.
The Interest Rate Parity Theorem.

that for Fisher Open. Investors shift funds to exploit any profit opportunity from deviations between the exchange agio and the interest agio; their transactions continue until there are no longer any unexploited profit opportunities.

For example, assume initially that interest rates on pengo-denominated Treasury Bills and dollar-denominated Treasury Bills are both 4 per cent; the Interest Rate Parity Theorem says that the price of the dollar in terms of the pengo in the forward market will be the same as the price in the spot market. Then interest rates on pengo Treasury Bills rise to 6 per cent. Investors are attracted by the higher interest rates on pengo Treasury Bills – they sell dollar Treasury Bills, purchase pengos in the spot exchange market and use the funds to buy pengo Treasury Bills. At the same time they sell pengos in the forward market, matching the maturity dates on the forward contracts with those on the pengo Treasury Bills. They anticipate that when the pengo Treasury Bills mature, the moneys received will be used to settle the forward contracts. The combination of the spot purchases and forward sales of the pengo protects investors from any loss from a depreciation of the pengo before their pengo investments mature. Investors continue to acquire short-term pengo assets as long as the discount on the forward pengo is less than 2 per cent; their transactions cause the pengo to appreciate in the spot market and to depreciate in the forward market, until the forward discount reaches 2 per cent. However, if arbitrage causes pengo interest rates to fall or dollar interest rates to rise, the post-disturbance equilibrium values for the exchange agio may be somewhat less than 2 per cent.

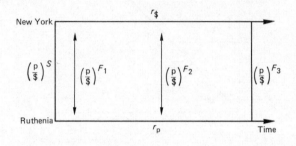

Fig. 3.5.
Equilibrium in the international money market.

Investors seek to equalise rates of return on domestic and foreign securities after covering themselves against any loss from changes in exchange rates. The transactions paths of investors are shown in Fig. 3.5. The return on dollar investments is shown in the top row, while the return on pengo investments is shown in the bottom row. Time is represented on the horizontal axis. The exchange rate – the pengo price of the dollar – is shown on the vertical axis; the spot exchange rate is at the left, while today's rates for near and distant maturities of forward contracts are to the right, with the more distant forward maturities further to the right. An investor based in New York might buy dollar investments and earn $r_\$$ per unit of time, or he might invest in pengos and earn r_p per unit of time. In the latter case he will not incur an exchange risk if he sells the pengo forward at the same time as he buys the pengo spot. Similarly, the investor based in Ruthenia might either buy pengo assets or dollar assets.[11] In equilibrium, the yields to investors in both New York and Ruthenia from holding dollar assets and pengo assets are the same after adjustment for the cost of hedging the exchange risk with forward contracts.

This example assumes that New York and Ruthenian investors arbitrage by shifting investments between deposits denominated in different currencies. Investors also arbitrage by altering the currencies in which they denominate their liabilities. Thus when Ruthenian interest rates rise relative to U.S. interest rates, some firms might borrow less in Ruthenia and borrow more in New York; to neutralise their exchange risk exposure, these firms would sell the pengo forward at the same time as they buy the pengo spot.

Forward rates would always be at the level suggested by the interest agios if arbitrage were a riskless and costless activity. In fact, forward rates frequently differ from the values predicted from the money-market interest agios. Transactions costs, generally no more than 0.1–0.2 per cent, can explain only a small part of the observed differentials between the actual forward rates and the predicted forward rates. Investors recognise that hedging the exchange risk does not eliminate all risk, for domestic and foreign securities are not perfect substitutes. Thus a New York-based investor might be concerned that he might not be able to repatriate his funds from Ruthenia at the conclusion of his investment because of the interim introduction of exchange controls.[12] Because of this risk, the investor might require a higher return on the foreign investment than on domestic investments. So the forward rate may differ from its interest parity. What appears as an unexploited profit opportunity represents the payment required for carrying political risk.

MONETARY DISTURBANCES AND THE PROPORTIONALITY PROPOSITIONS

The implication of the proportionality propositions is that changes in exchange rates reflect that the growth of the money supply in relation to the growth of money demand is more rapid in one country than in others, which leads to increases in both its commodity price levels and its interest rates. These propositions reflect long-run trend relationships.

Monetary policy is frequently managed as a short-term counter-cyclical instrument; central banks follow contractive policies to dampen inflationary booms and expansive policies to mitigate recessions. Counter-cyclical monetary policies cause the rates of money supply growth to vary from their trend levels. In a one-currency world, monetary expansion leads to a reduction in short-term interest rates as long as investors believe the commodity price level will be stable; monetary contraction, in contrast, is associated with an increase in interest rates. However, during the early stages of monetary expansion, interest rates may fall below the trend level; subsequently, interest rates rise to match the increase in the commodity price level.

In the multiple currency world, changes — and anticipated changes —

in the rate of money supply growth may have sharp impacts on the level of exchange rate. Purchasing Power Parity implies that the rate of change in the exchange rate is proportional to the difference in rates of change in national price levels, but the time dimension in which this relationship holds is not specified. Deviations from Purchasing Power Parity may occur, and reflect that 'arbitrage' between the goods markets in the several countries does not occur sufficiently rapidly to forestall deviations between changes in the exchange rate and changes in the ratio of national price levels.

If changes in monetary policy lead to changes in the anticipated exchange rates, then the current spot rate may change, and move to the 'discounted' values of the anticipated spot rates. Investors may buy foreign exchange in the forward market if the quoted forward rate, F_t, differs from the anticipated spot rate, S^*_{t+n}, by an amount sufficiently large to justify the risks. Arbitragers cause the differences between the forward exchange rates, F_t for various maturities, and the current spot rate, S_t, to equal the money market interest differentials, $r_d - r_f$, as suggested by Interest Rate Parity. Thus the anticipated spot exchange rates for various future dates, the current spot rate and the interest agios are linked by investors, as suggested by Fisher Open. Since the anticipated spot exchange rates, and hence the forward rates, are determined by the changes – or by anticipated changes – in monetary policy, while the foreign interest rate can be considered given, changes in the spot exchange rate in response to any change or anticipated change in monetary policy follow from its impacts on domestic interest rates and on the anticipated spot exchange rates.

Fig. 3.6 shows several models of the changes in the anticipated spot exchange rates and the forward exchange rates in response to changes in monetary policy. The exchange rate is measured on the vertical axis as pengos per dollar. Time is represented on the horizontal axis; the current date is t_0 and various future dates are shown to the right of t_0. Hence, at time t_0, the time profile of anticipated spot rates is shown as the vector S^*_{t+n}. Before the disturbance, the anticipated spot exchange rates for all future maturities are identical with the current spot rate.

Then Ruthenia adopts a more expansive monetary policy. If the Fisherian model holds, the time profile of the anticipated spot exchange rates will be represented by the positively sloped trajectory designated by the number one, and, as time passes, the spot rate will depreciate along this path – if there are no further disturbances. The change in monetary policy does not cause an immediate change in the level of the spot exchange rate, for consistency between the current spot exchange rate, the anticipated future spot rates and the foreign interest rate is realised by the one-time increase in the level of domestic interest rates. In the Fisherian model the increase in domestic interest rate for all maturities will be equal, in percentage points, to the anticipated rate of increase in the price level.

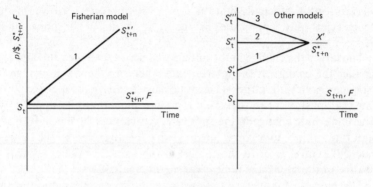

Fig. 3.6.
Changes in monetary policy and the exchange rate.

Several other models link the same change in monetary policy to the current spot exchange rate through the impact on the anticipated spot rate. These models differ from the Fisherian model in the assumptions about the impact of the monetary disturbance on either the interest rate, or the anticipated spot exchange rates. The several trajectories in the panel on the right in Fig. 3.6 indicate a less sharp increase in the interest rate than in the Fisherian model in response to Ruthenia's adoption of the identical expansive monetary policy. The common feature of the three models presented in the panel on the right, as well as in the Fisherian model, is that the anticipated spot rate, the domestic interest rate, the foreign interest rate and the current spot rate must be consistent with each other – otherwise there is an unexploited profit opportunity. Thus, if the domestic interest rate does not change as Ruthenia follows a more expansive monetary policy, even while the anticipated spot rate changes, then the spot rate must move immediately to its anticipated value, which is shown by trajectory 2. The adoption of the more expansive monetary policy leads to an immediate depreciation of the pengo from S_t to S''_t; for some time thereafter, the spot rate remains constant. If the domestic interest rates increase as Ruthenia follows the more expansive policy, but by less than in the Fisherian model, the spot exchange rate depreciates immediately to S'_t, and then depreciates along trajectory 1. If instead the pengo interest rate declines in response to the more expansive policy, the spot rate depreciates immediately to S'''_t, and then appreciates along trajectory 3 to the anticipated spot rate. The rationale is that if the rates of return on pengo and foreign securities are to be equal after adjustment for the change in the exchange rate, investors must anticipate that the pengo will appreciate. However, the pengo can only appreciate in the near future if it immediately depreciates.

The larger the change in the anticipated spot exchange rates and the smaller the change in the interest rate whenever there is a change in monetary policy, the larger is the immediate change in the spot exchange rate that must occur so that there is no unexploited profit opportunity. The immediate change in the spot rate, represented by the shift in the spot rate from S_t to S'_t or S''_t or S'''_t, was not suggested by the interest rate differential prior to the change in the monetary policy – but this change in the monetary policy was unanticipated.[13]

The impact of monetary expansion or monetary contraction in the long run must be reconciled with its impact in the short run. In the long run, the proportionality propositions hold; an increase in the rate of money supply growth relative to growth in money demand is associated with a higher interest rate and an increase in the price of foreign exchange. If, in the short run, an increase in money supply growth is associated with lower interest rates, the price of foreign exchange will increase sharply as investors associate the monetary expansion with an increase in domestic prices. Initially, the change in the exchange rate is sharper than the increase in the price of foreign exchange. Subsequently either the depreciation of the currency will be reversed, or price levels will begin to increase at a more rapid rate than the currency depreciates.

PROPORTIONALITY THEOREMS IN AN UNCERTAIN WORLD

The Quantity Theory of Money, the Purchasing Power Parity Theory, Fisher Closed and Fisher Open, and the Interest Rate Parity Theorem comprise a systematic view of international monetary relationships. Each involves a prediction. The outputs of one proposition are the inputs for the next in a logical fashion. The Quantity Theory predicts rates of change in the commodity price levels in each country, using the rates of growth of their money supplies as inputs, on the assumption that the demand for money in each country is constant. Purchasing Power Parity predicts rates of change in the exchange rates, using the differences in rates of change in the national price levels as the inputs, on the assumption that the impacts of structural change on the exchange rate are small or offsetting. Fisher Open predicts interest rate differentials, and hence the interest rate in each country, using the anticipated rates of change in the exchange rates as the inputs, on the assumption that the real interest rates in the several countries are constant. The Interest Rate Parity Theorem predicts forward exchange rates, using the interest rate differentials as the inputs, on the assumption that there are no significant exchange controls on shifts of funds across countries.

Assume, for example, that the Ruthenian price level is increasing at a constant rate of 10 per cent a year, while the U.S. price level remains constant. Purchasing Power Parity 'predicts' that the price of the dollar in terms of the pengo should increase at the rate of 10 per cent a year. If the anticipated real interest rates in the United States and Ruthenia are the same, Fisher Closed predicts that the money rate of interest in Ruthenia should be 10 percentage points higher than the money rate of interest in the United States.[14] Fisher Open provides the same prediction. The Interest Rate Parity Theorem predicts that the pengo should be at a forward discount of 10 per cent a year for all forward maturities. Whenever the actual values differ from the predicted values, there is an apparent profit opportunity, at least in a riskless world. If interest rates on pengo-denominated bonds are less than 10 percentage points higher than those on dollar bonds, investors would sell the pengo bonds and buy dollar bonds. The interest rates on pengo bonds would increase, and dollar interest rates might decline, until the interest agio adjusts to the anticipated rate of change in the exchange rate. Similarly, if the discount on the forward pengo is either larger or smaller than 10 per cent, investors would engage in covered interest arbitrage to exploit the riskless profit opportunity.

One implication of this set of logical relationships is that changes in exchange rates can be predicted using information on the changes in the money supply—money demand relationship in the several countries as the inputs. A second, less obvious implication is that opportunities to profit on a systematic basis from the forthcoming changes in exchange rates by altering the currency mix of assets and liabilities should not arise if the interest agio or the forward exchange rates predict the forthcoming changes in exchange rates; in both cases, the scope for profitable speculation has been eliminated. Systematic profits from changes in exchange rates can be earned only if the interest agio or the forward exchange rates do not fully predict the anticipated spot exchange rates. The opportunity to secure systematic profits from anticipated changes in the exchange rates requires that investors have superior skills in estimating the exchange rate consequences of future monetary disturbances – or in identifying the likelihood of such disturbances in the future.

In a world of both monetary and non-monetary disturbances, both economic and political, these concepts must be tested to determine whether they are empirically valid. Some of the anticipated changes in exchange rates may occur; some may not. The rates of monetary expansion at home and abroad are affected by political factors, and so anticipations of changes in exchange rates require views on future monetary policies in the several countries and on the political forces bearing on these policies. Deviations between the predicted exchange rates for various dates inferred from the interest agios and the observed exchange rates on these dates result from imperfections in investor foresight. The empirical question is whether these deviations are random or systematic, and if systematic, why the profit opportunities have not been competed away.

The usefulness of this systematic structure for predicting changes in exchange rates depends on whether the implicit assumptions about lags, structural change, transactions costs and barriers are valid. Individuals may adjust their expenditures to changes in their money holdings with variable lags. Bureaucratic regulation may interfere with the operation of market forces. Exchange controls may insulate changes in interest rates in one national financial market from those in foreign markets. Changes in the demand for foreign goods may lag changes in domestic prices.

Whether these factors are significant can be determined by testing the empirical content of each of the propositions. The questions to be answered include whether there are systematic forecast errors, whether changes in exchange rates are inconsistent with Purchasing Power Parity, and whether there are better predictors of future spot exchange rates than current forward rates. A third question involves the confidence to place in each prediction; the concern is the distinction between the statement that on average – over a large number of observations – there are no systematic errors in the predictions, and the statement that the error in each prediction is smaller than that from other forecasts.

The formation of expectations about exchange rates may not follow the sequence of the proportionality propositions, which goes from changes in money supply to changes in exchange rates to interest rate differentials to the forward rate. Investors will seek to anticipate the impact of current – and possible – monetary policies on the future exchange rates. Hence the forward rates may approximate the anticipated spot exchange rates. The forward rates and the spot rates would necessarily be linked by money-market interest rate differential. In this way anticipations of changes in monetary policy might lead to changes in the spot exchange rate, even before the domestic price level changes. Hence the spot exchange rates might vary significantly as anticipations of monetary policy change and might differ from the levels suggested by Purchasing Power Parity.

Conceivably there might be systematic differences between the predicted exchange rates and the observed exchange rates that cannot be explained by institutional factors like transactions costs and taxes. Deviations between anticipated and observed exchange rates might be explained by exchange market phenomena, which cause the anticipated exchange rates to differ from the values suggested by changes in commodity price levels, or by capital market phenomena, which cause the interest rates to differ from the levels suggested by changes in commodity price levels. Whenever exchange rates are pegged, the observed exchange rates may differ from the levels suggested by changes in commodity price levels. What must be explained, however, is not why these deviations arise, but why they are not exploited by profit-maximising entrepreneurs so that they quickly disappear.

In the multi-currency world, borrowers may be reluctant to denominate debt in foreign currencies unless the reduction in their interest costs more than compensates the risk of loss from unanticipated changes in the exchange rate. Similarly, lenders may be reluctant to hold assets denominated in currencies whose foreign exchange value is continually changing because they are uncertain about the future purchasing power of these assets in terms of the goods they will ultimately consume. Residents in each country would normally prefer to hold assets denominated in their domestic currencies because the prices of most of their consumption goods are expressed in the domestic currency. Any preference for matching the currency mix of their investment assets with the 'currency mix of the consumption goods' might restrain investors from acquiring assets denominated in currencies which offer higher interest rates, even after adjustment for the anticipated changes in exchange rates. To the extent investors are uncertain about future exchange rates and prefer to hold assets denominated in certain currencies, systematic errors might arise between the predictions of future exchange rates inferred from both the interest agio and the exchange agio, and the observed exchange rates on the maturity of the predictions. A currency premium might develop; the interest agio and the exchange agio would show systematic biases in their predictions of future spot exchange rates.[15] That an *a priori* argument can be made for a currency premium does not, however, mean that such premia are observable.

Investors are likely to be more uncertain about the future foreign exchange value of some currencies than of others, in part because their confidence in the stability of the monetary policies in various countries differs. Thus they may be more uncertain about the future value of sterling than of the Canadian dollar. Moreover, investors may have much less confidence about the future exchange rates for distant maturities than for near maturities.

Uncertainty about future monetary policies might explain why investors have currency preferences. The *a priori* argument against currency preferences is that any systematic differential between the predicted exchange rate and the exchange rate at which investors would be indifferent between holding securities denominated in the several currencies would represent an unexploited profit opportunity, which would attract risk-neutral investors who would compete away the unusually high profits.

Finally, even if investors are risk-averse and concerned to minimise the variations in their income that might arise as a result of unanticipated changes in exchange rate, they would evaluate their holdings of assets and liabilities denominated in each foreign currency in terms of its contribution to their total income. Changes in the price of the dollar in terms of various foreign currencies are not perfectly correlated with each other, although the correlations of changes of currencies within each of the several currency areas – the mark area, the French franc area, and the sterling area – are high. The implication is that the more diversified the foreign exchange holdings of an individual risk-averse investor, the smaller the premium that may be required to induce him to add to his position in any one currency, because he is concerned with the risk in all currencies together.

SUMMARY

Interest rate differentials and forward exchange rates can be considered as forecasts of exchange rates at various future dates if changes in exchange rates are primarily a monetary phenomenon. In this event, changes in domestic price levels, the exchange rate, interest rates and forward exchange rates are logically related. The activities of arbitragers who seek any unexploited profit opportunity would ensure that the logical relationships prevail.

4. Political Risk and International Investment

Political risk involves the uncertainty that investors have about changes in laws and regulations that national authorities apply to the transfer of funds across national borders and the ownership of assets within their jurisdictions by foreign firms and residents. Each national government can control the movement of securities across national borders, thus hindering foreign loans and investments, and the repatriation of profits, dividends and capital. Each government can use its legal powers to acquire the property of private parties – of foreign residents as well as of domestic residents – located within its jurisdiction. And each also can refuse to pay its debts to foreigners with minimal fear of being sued.

In many countries the conduct of day-to-day business requires government licences or permits – building licences, import licences, zoning variances and employment permits. Foreign firms may find these licences more difficult to obtain than their domestic competitors; they may be subject to a more restrictive set of regulations than domestic residents are. Some governments may discriminate in the regulations applied to domestic affiliates of various foreign firms, depending on the country of domicile of the parents. While governments may bind themselves to avoid such discriminatory practices, they are displaced by elections, wars and revolutions, and the successor regimes may not honour the debts, commitments and obligations of their predecessors.

The concern with political risk affects the decisions of firms about where to invest and how to finance their foreign activities. Political risk tends to segment national capital markets from the international capital market. Interest rates on similar assets available in various countries differ because investors demand a payment for carrying political risk.[1] This interest rate differential must be compared with the losses that firms incur both because of the various government interferences with the movement of funds abroad and of expropriation; the data bearing on this comparison are discussed in Chapter 7.

POLITICAL RISK AND FINANCIAL ASSETS

Traditionally, the separation of investors' assessments of political risk from their assessments of exchange risk has been arbitrary, for the interest rate differential jointly includes payments demanded by investors for carrying both risks. The growth of the Euro-currency and Euro-bond markets facilitates a sharper evaluation of political risk on similar financial assets issued in various centres.[2] These markets involve the issue of liabilities in various centres – principally London, Zürich, Frankfurt, Luxembourg and Singapore – denominated in currencies other than that of the country in which the transaction occurs. For example, many banks in London – the London branches of U.S. and of Swiss banks as well as British banks – issue deposits denominated in U.S. dollars; these deposits share the exchange risk attribute of dollar deposits issued in the United States but not their political risk attribute. Dollar deposits issued in London, like sterling deposits produced there, are primarily within the regulatory jurisdiction of the British banking authorities.[3]

The growth of offshore financial markets is a response to government regulation of financial transactions in domestic financial markets. Transactions are less extensively regulated in the offshore market than in the domestic markets; offshore deposits are not subject to interest rate ceilings, and banks generally are not required to hold reserves against their external currency deposits.[4] Indeed, if offshore transactions are significantly regulated they become non-competitive, and so the transactions would be shifted to the centres which are freer of regulation.

A lender contemplating a choice between dollar deposits in London and dollar deposits in New York is not concerned with exchange risk; his net worth would be unaffected by change in the sterling–dollar exchange rate. This investor is concerned with political risk, for British authorities may apply exchange controls to London dollar deposits, perhaps similar to those applied to sterling deposits, which might delay or prevent the shift of dollar funds from Great Britain. The authorities could issue directives to the banks which have issued these dollar deposits, instructing them not to permit their withdrawal, or the authorities might issue directives to the owners of these deposits, prohibiting the removal of these funds from British jurisdiction. Similarly, the U.S. authorities might apply exchange controls to the flow of dollars from the United States.

Deposits produced in London and Zürich and other financial centres might be denominated in any foreign currency as an alternative to the domestic currency.[5] Currently there are fewer than ten currencies in which the exchange risk and political risk attributes of financial assets are readily segmented, and there are only three currencies – the dollar, the mark and the Swiss franc – in which the volume of external currency deposits is large.[6]

		Country of issue				
		United States	Great Britain	Germany	Spain	Brazil
Currency of denomination	Dollars	New York Dollars	London Dollars	Frankfurt Dollars		
	Sterling		London Sterling	Frankfurt Sterling		
	Mark		London Mark	Frankfurt Mark		
	Peseta				Madrid Peseta	
	Cruzeiro					Rio Cruzeiro

Fig. 4.1.
International money market assets.

The set of money market assets available in a five-country, five-currency world is shown in Fig. 4.1. New York dollar deposits differ from London sterling deposits in terms of both exchange risk and political risk. New York dollar deposits differ from London dollar deposits solely in terms of political risk. Similarly, London sterling deposits differ from New York sterling deposits in terms of political risk.

The traditional assets in international finance, those denominated in the currency of the country in which they are issued, are shown in the cells on the northwest–southeast diagonal. The external currency assets are identified in other cells. The shaded cells indicate external currency assets that are not yet readily available; however, these assets could be easily produced if it were profitable to do so.

The dimensions of political risk vary with the type of exchange controls that might be applied by authorities in different countries to assets produced in their jurisdictions. Investor attitude towards the riskiness of particular assets can be inferred from the interest rates available on these assets. In the absence of political risk, interest rates on the various assets identified in the matrix would differ only because of exchange risk – the interest rates on the assets in each of the several rows might differ, even though the interest rates in the several cells would be identical within each row. In contrast, in the absence of exchange risk, the interest rates on the assets identified in the matrix would differ because of political risk – the interest rates would be uniform within each column, and possibly different across columns. Moreover, if investors believe that the authorities within a country might apply one set of controls to assets denominated in the domestic currency and another set to assets denominated in various foreign currencies, then interest rates on the assets within the several rows in each column might differ.

Four dimensions of risk can be highlighted with the matrix. One involves the comparison between New York dollars and London sterling – between securities issued in different countries denominated in their domestic currencies. A second involves the comparison between New York dollars and London dollars – between securities issued in domestic banking centres and offshore centres denominated in the same currency. A third involves the comparison between London dollars and London marks – between securities issued in the same offshore centre denominated in various foreign currencies. A fourth involves the comparison between London dollars and Zürich dollars – between securities issued in various offshore centres denominated in the same foreign currency.

Investors continually compare the risks and returns on assets available in different financial centres. The New York dollars–London sterling comparison involves the risk that the authorities within either country might apply exchange controls to deposits denominated in its own currency, and delay or prevent the movement of funds to a foreign currency or to a foreign financial centre. The comparison between New York dollars and London dollars involves the risk that the British authorities might apply controls to movements of funds denominated in a foreign currency from the domestic financial centre to a foreign centre – and that the U.S. authorities might apply controls to the outflow of dollars. On an *a priori* basis, the authorities in each country appear less likely to apply controls to deposits denominated in foreign currencies than to deposits denominated in their own currency, on the rationale that movements of funds denominated in foreign currencies are not likely to constrain the management of the country's monetary policy or affect its international reserve position or its exchange rate. Transactions in foreign currencies provide an opportunity to earn income from providing banking services to non-residents. The greater the likelihood that particular transactions might be controlled, the greater the political risk. Consequently, the differential in interest rates that can be attributed to political risk should be greater when the comparison involves two domestic currency deposits, such as New York dollars and London sterling, than when it involves a domestic currency deposit and an external currency deposit denominated in the same currency.[7]

The political risk attached to external deposits denominated in various currencies issued in one offshore banking centre should be distinguished from the political risk attached to external deposits denominated in any one currency issued in different offshore centres. In the first case, investors can choose among external deposits in London denominated in dollars, marks and Swiss francs. The political risk attached to these deposits might differ if investors believe that regulations applied to external deposits denominated in one or several foreign currencies would differ from those applied to external deposits in some other currencies. Yet there is no rationale, logical or otherwise, which suggests why the authorities should discriminate among transactions in different foreign currencies.

Investors are necessarily concerned with the political risk attached to external deposits denominated in the same currency and available in different countries; they continually evaluate the merits of dollar deposits in London, Zürich, Madrid, São Paulo, even Moscow on the likelihood that the authorities in one centre or another might adopt regulations that would make it difficult 'to get their money out'. The traditions of bureaucratic regulation in Moscow and São Paulo seem so strong that it appears highly risky to hold dollar or Swiss franc deposits in either place – unless the yields are much higher than on dollar deposits in London and Zürich. That the major centres of offshore banking are London, Zürich, Luxembourg and Singapore is not an accident, for the authorities in these countries have established traditions of minimal interference in financial transactions, especially for 'entrepôt' activities like offshore banking.

At any moment, the interest rates on dollar deposits available in London, Zürich and other offshore centres are virtually identical. Most financial intermediaries – the banks that produce these deposits – have no financial incentive to pay a higher interest rate to sell dollar deposits in one centre if they can sell dollar deposits at a lower interest rate in any other foreign centre. No offshore bank would pay higher interest rates on dollar deposits in Zürich or Moscow than in London.[8] These banks sell offshore dollars in the centres which investors believe least subject to political risk; these investors are price-takers and adjust their demands for deposits in each currency in these various centres as their assessment of the various risks changes. Thus if investors perceive that the risk of holding dollar deposits in Paris has risen relative to that of holding dollar deposits in other offshore centres, their demand for Paris dollar deposits will decline, even as the constellation of interest rates on offshore deposits remains unchanged. The centres deemed least risky are those with the larger shares of total offshore deposits.[9]

Investors continuously compare the interest rates on deposits with different combinations of exchange risk and political risk; they seek deposits which have interest rates which are high relative to their estimates of the associated risks. Thus the interest rates on each type of deposit reflect the investors' estimates of the associated risks. The higher the interest rates on London sterling deposits relative to those on New York dollar deposits, the stronger the investor anticipation that sterling might depreciate or that the British authorities might tighten their controls on outflows of sterling funds.

Whether investors believe that differential regulation is likely can be inferred from the relationship between the interest agios on these deposits denominated in dollars, sterling and marks, and the exchange agios. If the interest agios and exchange agios differ by no more than the transactions costs – i.e. the Interest Rate Parity Theorem holds for external deposits denominated in different currencies – then it can be inferred that investors believe they do not differ from each other in terms of political risk.[10]

The difference between the interest agios on domestic deposits dominated in various currencies and the exchange agios represents the payment demanded by investors for carrying the political risk on domestic deposits. If investors attach greater political risk to London sterling deposits than to New York dollar deposits, there will be systematic deviations from interest rate parity; interest rates on London sterling deposits will exceed those on New York dollar deposits by more than the anticipated depreciation of sterling, as inferred from the forward exchange rates.[11]

A comparison of the interest rates on external and domestic deposits denominated in any currency indicates the payment that the marginal investor receives as he alters his exposure to political risk. The spread between domestic and external interest rates on dollar deposits has generally been less volatile than the comparable spreads for deposits denominated in other currencies. Dollar-denominated deposits account for three-quarters of external deposits; the variations in the spread between domestic and offshore dollar deposits can be considered the market effect and generally follow variations in monetary ease and tightness in the United States. In addition, the interest rates on external deposits denominated in all currencies other than the dollar show a country effect, which is reflected in variations in the forward discount or premium on that country's currency.

An analogy may be drawn between investor concern with changes in exchange rates and changes in exchange controls. One view is that forward exchange rates are unbiased predictors of the future spot rates. While the variance between the predicted exchange rates and the observed exchange rates may be large, the difference between the mean of the predicted spot rates and the mean of the observed rates on the dates when the predictions mature may not be statistically different from zero. The analogy is that the component of the interest rate differential associated with possible changes in exchange controls is an unbiased predictor of the losses that investors might incur as a result of tightening of exchange controls, both on domestic deposits issued in various centres and on external deposits in various currencies. The rationale for this view is that competition among investors should keep this component in line with the anticipated losses attributable to changes in exchange controls and the risk of such changes; otherwise there would be an unexploited profit opportunity. While the variance between the predicted loss and the observed loss may be large, the difference between the mean of the political risk premiums and the observed loss from exchange controls would not be statistically significant after investors are rewarded for bearing the uncertainty. Alternatively, the data might show that investors receive an excessive payment for subjecting themselves to political risk.

Determining whether payment for bearing political risk is excessive is more complicated than determining whether there is a currency premium. Because of the selective nature of changes in exchange controls, estimating the gains or losses attributable to changes in exchange controls is more difficult than measuring the gains or losses attributable to changes in exchange rates.

POLITICAL RISK AND NON-FINANCIAL ASSETS

The expropriation of local properties of U.S. oil companies in the Middle East, of the U.S. copper companies in Chile, and of Dutch companies in Indonesia indicates why investors are so concerned with political risk. International investors have long been aware that special risks were attached to ownership of assets abroad. Consequently, the threshold return on foreign investment has been higher than that on domestic investments to compensate for the additional risks. Investors have sought to borrow from host-country sources to reduce the probable loss they might incur upon expropriation. The expectation is that if the host-country government were to take over the local subsidiary, the parent would not be obliged to repay the debts of the subsidiary, so its loss would be limited to its own investments in the subsidiary or those that it had guaranteed. The interest cost of host-country borrowing was usually higher, and so the question to be answered is whether the cumulative value of the difference in interest costs is high or low relative to the losses that firms have incurred as a result of expropriation and similar political decisions.

Financial markets in some countries may be so underdeveloped that the foreign firms are not able to reduce their exposure substantially by borrowing within the host countries. In the Middle East, Latin America and elsewhere the petroleum companies finance their payments for concessions from external sources. These firms adjust to the risks of partial or total expropriation by altering the size of their bids for the concessions to explore for oil; the higher their perception of the probable loss from expropriation, the lower their bids. The firms anticipate they will recover the costs of bearing the risk in the price at which they will sell the commodity in the world market.

Ideally, a set of 'actuarial tables' might be developed for losses from expropriation. If data were available, a comparison could be made between the decline in the firm's income stream as a result of the political acts of host governments, with the increase in its income from its willingness to take on the risks of these foreign investments. While individual firms probably make estimates of this trade-off, comprehensive data for groups of firms are not available.

A long time series of interest rates on financial assets produced in different countries is available, so the cumulative income from carrying the risk of losses from exchange controls could be computed. However, no estimates of the returns required by investors for increasing their exposure to risks of expropriation are available. Whether the yield differentials and the profit rates are sufficiently high to compensate the occasional losses due to expropriation or whether firms are excessively cautious, so that there are unexploited profit opportunities, is unclear.[12] The experiences with expropriation have been so infrequent that developing a systematic approach to the calculation of probable loss from future expropriations seems unlikely to be successful.

SUMMARY

Political risk involves the uncertainty about possible losses from the application of a variety of government controls to financial and non-financial assets held by foreign investors. The number of possible controls is high – the governments may restrict the transfer of funds, reduce the prospective income by taxes, licences or administrative fiat, or expropriate wealth. Investors must attempt to forecast the likelihood of such controls and their costs. The prospect of controls tends to increase the costs or reduce the profits anticipated on foreign investments; as a consequence, yields on assets available within the countries likely to apply these controls are probably higher than those available elsewhere. Whether the yield differentials are high or low relative to the losses from these controls and expropriation has not yet been resolved.

5. Changes in Exchange Rates and National Commodity Price Levels

Three proportionality concepts – the Purchasing Power Parity Theory, Fisher Open and the Interest Rate Parity Theorem – involve the relationships between changes in exchange rates and levels and rates of change of national commodity price levels, interest agios and exchange agios. If these propositions are continuously valid in the short run as well as in the long run, exchange risk disappears; the firm's net worth, income and market value would not be affected by changes in exchange rates, regardless of the currencies in which its assets and liabilities are denominated.[1] To the extent that there are deviations from these propositions, either in the short run or the long run, changes in exchange rates may affect the firm's income and perhaps its market value.

Many firms base their strategies on the currency mix of their assets and liabilities on assumptions – more or less implicit – about these relationships. Hence a test of these assumptions in effect tests the empirical content of their strategies.[2] A central question is the relationship between changes in the relative price levels and changes in the exchange rates over many countries and over an extended interval; the related question involves the frequency and extent of deviations from Purchasing Power Parity in the short run.

This chapter examines the empirical validity of the Purchasing Power Parity Theory, while the next chapter considers the same issue about Fisher Open. Deviations between predicted and observed values are not unexpected, since the world is subject to shocks and change, and foresight is imperfect. One of the key questions is whether these deviations are random or whether they are systematic. A second is whether the deviations in the short run differ significantly from those in the long run and the operational meaning and implications of the distinction between the short run and the long run.

55

CHANGES IN EXCHANGE RATES, INDIVIDUAL PRICES AND THE COMMODITY PRICE LEVEL

The implication of the Purchasing Power Parity Theory for the firm is that the local currency prices of plant and equipment and of inventories change on a one-for-one basis with changes in exchange rates. Examination of the deviations from Purchasing Power Parity should indicate how the firm's net worth and income would be affected by changes in exchange rates if it holds non-monetary assets in countries whose currencies have depreciated or appreciated. Purchasing Power Parity is necessarily aggregative; changes in the commodity price level within any country may obscure somewhat offsetting changes in several of its components. While information would be desirable about the relationship between changes in exchange rates and changes in the local currency prices of particular non-monetary assets owned by individual firms, there is no *a priori* reason why changes in the commodity price level should be a biased indicator of changes in the local currency prices of the particular assets owned by these firms. Consequently, information about the changes in the commodity price level is a useful first approximation to changes in the prices of particular assets included in the index.

The Purchasing Power Parity Theory is a proposition about the long-term equilibrium relationships between changes in relative commodity price levels and changes in the equilibrium exchange rate. The firm is interested in a related but different question – to what extent do the changes in exchange rates occur without corresponding changes in relative commodity price levels, either contemporaneously or with a lag. Even if all changes in the relationships between commodity price levels lead to proportional changes in the equilibrium exchange rate, it does not follow that all changes in exchange rates reflect changes in relative commodity price levels; instead some may reflect structural changes.

The test of Purchasing Power Parity is whether the ratio of changes in national commodity price levels to changes in exchange rates – the ratio of changes in relative commodity price levels to changes in relative currency prices – approximates 1, where

$$\text{Percentage deviation from Purchasing Power Parity} = \left(\frac{\dfrac{P_{f,t}/P_{f,t-1}}{P_{d,t}/P_{d,t-1}}}{E_t/E_{t-1} - 1} \right) \times 100$$

$P_{f,t;f,t-1}$ = foreign commodity price level at times t and $t-1$;

$P_{d,t;d,t-1}$ = domestic commodity price level at times t and $t-1$;

$E_{t;t-1}$ = exchange rate at times t and $t-1$ expressed as the number of foreign currency units per domestic currency unit.

Several questions arise in applying the concept. One involves determining the maximum deviation that is not inconsistent with Purchasing Power Parity.[3] For example, the commodity price level of one country may increase more rapidly than the price levels in other countries, without any changes in the exchange rate between their currencies, perhaps because the components of their price level indexes are not identical or because transport costs limit arbitrage between the goods markets in the several countries. Deviations from Purchasing Power Parity associated with changes in exchange rates may be compared with the deviations that occur when the exchange rates between their currencies are unchanged; the latter deviations provide minimum estimates of deviations attributable to factors other than changes in exchange rates.

A second operational question in the application of Purchasing Power Parity involves the selection of the price level indexes and the exchange rates to use in computing the ratio; the indexes which might be used include those for consumer goods, or the cost of living, wholesale goods, export goods, import goods, tradeable goods (export and import goods together) and the GNP deflator. Several different exchange rates can be used to compute the ratio, including the parity or the market rate and the black market rate. The data used in measuring the deviations in this chapter are the consumer price indexes and the parity exchange rates or the market rates.[4]

DEVIATIONS FROM PURCHASING POWER PARITY: THE LONG RUN

Price and exchange rate data for nearly fifty countries were examined for the period since 1950. Countries were placed into four groups in Table 5.1 on the basis of their exchange rate histories. Group I includes countries which did not change their currency parities relative to the U.S. dollar during the observation period; Group II, countries which devalued their currencies; Group III, countries which revalued; and Group IV, countries which both devalued and revalued or allowed their currencies to float for an extended period.[5]

TABLE 5.1 Deviations from Purchasing Power Parity

Terminal year	Mean annual average					Absolute annual average				
	Initial year					*Initial year*				
	1950	1955	1960	1965	1970	1950	1955	1960	1965	1970
	GROUP I									
1955	0.26					0.40				
1960	−0.97	−2.14				0.97	2.14			
1965	−0.23	−0.46	1.29			0.93	1.43	1.34		
1970	−0.54	−0.78	−0.13	−1.40		0.58	0.80	0.38	1.40	
1975	−0.69	−0.92	−0.31	−0.51	1.12	0.69	0.92	0.31	0.51	1.44
	GROUP II									
1955	−2.20					4.47				
1960	−1.00	0.19				1.95	2.43			
1965	−0.79	−0.11	−0.63			2.28	2.55	2.90		
1970	−0.91	−0.54	−0.85	−1.13		1.55	1.16	1.68	3.00	
1975	−0.76	−0.39	−0.60	−0.60	0.73	1.20	0.65	0.99	1.37	2.92
	GROUP III									
1955	2.46					2.69				
1960	0.89	−0.65				1.29	0.73			
1965	1.12	0.39	1.48			1.17	0.53	1.54		
1970	0.80	0.22	0.68	−0.13		0.88	0.50	0.88	0.57	
1975	1.46	1.07	1.69	1.76	3.64	1.46	1.07	1.72	1.77	3.64

TABLE 5.1 (*continued*)

Terminal year	Initial year — Mean annual average					Initial year — Absolute annual average				
	1950	1955	1960	1965	1970	1950	1955	1960	1965	1970
GROUP IV										
1955	5.05					6.85				
1960	3.04	0.65				4.34	3.09			
1965	1.74	0.95	1.03			2.63	2.35	2.90		
1970	0.95	0.11	−0.17	4.10		1.70	1.32	0.93	6.74	
1975	0.92	0.11	0.51	0.29	1.75	1.54	0.81	1.35	0.93	2.07
GROUPS I–IV										
1955	2.57					4.32				
1960	1.36	−0.01				2.58	2.05			
1965	0.92	0.47	0.81			1.83	1.62	2.22		
1970	0.45	−0.03	−0.06	1.73		1.22	0.92	0.92	4.09	
1975	0.55	0.18	0.48	0.40	1.67	1.08	0.70	1.01	0.93	2.06

Source: *International Financial Statistics.*

TABLE 5.2 Deviations from Purchasing Power Parity: Major U.S. Trading Partners

Terminal year	Wholesale prices — Initial year					Consumer prices — Initial year				
	1950	1955	1960	1965	1970	1950	1955	1960	1965	1970
TOP FIVE										
1955	1.54					2.29				
1960	0.35	−0.79				1.24	0.13			
1965	0.65	0.18	1.20			1.70	1.33	2.52		
1970	0.42	0.05	0.51	−0.14		1.24	0.77	1.10	−0.29	
1975	0.81	0.58	1.11	1.02	2.17	2.29	1.87	2.44	2.02	4.28
SECOND FIVE										
1955	−0.82					0.45				
1960	−0.96	−1.26				0.29	−0.22			
1965	−0.53	−0.52	0.21			0.07	−0.27	0.23		
1970	−0.43	−0.27	0.25	0.31		−0.29	−0.26	−0.20	−0.28	
1975	−0.12	0.02	0.49	0.58	0.96	0.80	0.82	1.22	1.74	3.98
THIRD FIVE										
1955	2.16					1.65				
1960	0.97	−0.17				1.20	0.60			
1965	0.75	−0.10	0.14			0.96	0.36	0.07		
1970	0.27	−0.47	−0.51	−1.52		0.48	−0.11	−0.48	−1.58	
1975	0.97	0.51	0.78	1.32	5.06	2.15	1.95	2.35	2.98	8.02

TABLE 5.2 (continued)

Terminal year	Wholesale prices — Initial year					Consumer prices — Initial year				
	1950	1955	1960	1965	1970	1950	1955	1960	1965	1970
	TOP FIFTEEN									
1955	0.96					1.28				
1960	0.12	−0.74				0.81	0.17			
1965	0.29	−0.15	0.52			0.79	0.47	0.79		
1970	0.09	−0.23	0.08	−0.45		0.41	0.14	0.14	−0.72	
1975	0.49	0.34	0.74	0.89	2.39	1.54	1.55	2.00	2.25	5.43

Source: *International Financial Statistics.*

One test of Purchasing Power Parity is the cumulative annual average deviations between predicted exchange rates and observed exchange rates over a period of five to ten years or longer. The significance of the observed deviation depends in part on whether the values for the price levels and exchange rates in the base years and the terminal years are equilibrium values. If 1950 is a disequilibrium base year (the large devaluations in September 1949 might have led to an overvalued dollar), the inferences derived using 1960 as a base year may be more meaningful. In general, any change in the deviation caused by varying the base or terminal year is small because the change is averaged over a large number of years.[6]

Table 5.1 shows the average annual rates of deviation from Purchasing Power Parity for countries in each of these four groups, and for the 44 countries together, for various five-year periods, beginning in 1950 and ending in 1975. The countries in each group have equal weights in computing the average weights. A minus entry means that the foreign price level fell relative to the U.S. price level after adjustment for the change in the exchange rate.

The dominant impression is that the average annual rates of deviation are modest – for most five-year intervals, less than 2 per cent a year. The average annual rates of deviation for countries in Group II and Group IV are about the same as those for countries in Group I; those for Group III are somewhat larger but still reasonably small, with the exception of the rates of deviation in the most recent five-year period. In general, lengthening the interval of observation from five to ten years or longer reduces the values for the average annual rates of deviation. The absolute values for the average annual rates are modestly larger for the Group I, II and IV countries, indicating that the low values for the average annual rates do not reflect the net of large positive and large negative values.

Table 5.2 shows the average annual rates of deviation for the fifteen most important U.S. trading partners, grouped by the top five, the second five and the third five, using both consumer and wholesale price indexes. The data suggest inferences similar to those drawn from Table 5.1. The average annual rates of deviation are low for most intervals, with the largest average annual rates in the most recent five-year period. Lengthening the interval reduces the average annual rates of deviation. Rates of deviation based on the consumer price indexes are usually modestly larger than those based on the wholesale price indexes.

DEVIATIONS FROM PURCHASING POWER PARITY: THE SHORT RUN

The conclusion that deviations from Purchasing Power Parity are modest for intervals of five years or longer may not satisfy managers of firms who are concerned with the validity of the concept on a yearly basis. Their concern is with the maximum deviation from Purchasing Power Parity in shorter intervals and with the frequency of large deviations.

Both before and after changes in exchange parities, deviations from Purchasing Power Parity are likely to be substantial. Prior to the devaluation of a country's currency its commodity price level is likely to rise relative to the world commodity price level; the deviation between the observed exchange rate and the predicted exchange rate may increase as long as the parity remains unchanged. The change in the parity is almost certain to be larger than the contemporary change in relative price levels, and so the deviation would then be reversed. Similarly, casual observation suggests that month-to-month or year-to-year change in the foreign exchange value of a currency which floats freely may exceed the change suggested by changes in relative national price levels during the corresponding interval.

Table 5.3 shows the distribution of deviations from Purchasing Power Parity using both wholesale and consumer price indexes for intervals varying from one to five years for the fifteen most important U.S.

TABLE 5.3 Distribution of Deviations from Purchasing Power Parity

Length of intervals	Annual average deviation				No. of observations
	$<\pm2.5\%$	$<\pm5\%$	$<\pm10\%$	$<\pm25\%$	
	WHOLESALE PRICES				
1 year	31	66	86	97	374
2 years	37	74	91	99	359
3 years	41	81	95	100	344
4 years	43	83	97	100	329
5 years	50	87	98	100	314
	CONSUMER PRICES				
1 year	33	70	88	97	370
2 years	35	74	90	99	355
3 years	38	74	94	100	340
4 years	42	79	94	100	325
5 years	43	82	97	100	310

trading partners over the last twenty five years. Thus, 31 per cent of the deviations for one-year intervals are smaller than 2.5 per cent using wholesale prices; 66 per cent of the one-year deviations are smaller than 5 per cent. Similarly, 86 per cent of the deviations are less than 10 per cent on the basis of a one-year interval using the wholesale price indexes; as the interval is lengthened to five years, the percentage of deviations less than 10 per cent increases to 98 per cent. 87 per cent of the deviations are smaller than 5 per cent when the interval is five years. Lengthening the interval of observation always reduces the percentage of deviations in excess of a given amount. For intervals of three to four years or more, about four-fifths of the deviations are less than 5 per cent a year.

SUMMARY

This chapter has examined the relationship between changes in exchange rates and changes in relative commodity price levels. Whereas Purchasing Power Parity suggests that changes in relative price levels would lead to changes in exchange rates, changes in exchange rates might also reflect non-monetary or structural factors. The price level–exchange rate relationship was examined for nearly fifty countries for the 1950–75 period. For all countries the mean annual average deviation was 0.55 per cent a year, while the absolute annual deviation was slightly over 1 per cent. The deviations were largest for the countries whose currencies appreciated relative to the dollar, and especially in the 1970–5 quinquennium.

The price level–exchange rate relationship was also examined for the fifteen most important U.S. trading partners for intervals varying from one to five years. On an annual basis, using wholesale price data, 14 per cent of the deviations exceeded 10 per cent; over a five-year interval, only 2 per cent of the deviations exceeded 10 per cent and only 13 per cent exceeded 5 per cent. The data do not deny that Purchasing Power Parity is valid for a period approaching five years or longer. While most deviations for intervals of one and two years are less than 2.5 per cent a year, the percentage of larger deviations is sufficiently high for it to seem risky to conclude that Purchasing Power Parity will be valid in these shorter intervals. As the interval of observation is extended to three and four years, the large annual deviations are averaged and begin to approximate the average annual rates of deviation in the long run. The frequency of large deviations decreases as the interval of observation is lengthened.

6. Changes in Exchange Rates and Yield Differentials

Whether investors find it attractive to alter the currency mix of financial assets and liabilities in anticipation of changes in the exchange rates depends on how fully interest rate differentials and forward exchange rates reflect such anticipations. If Fisher Open holds continuously, changes in the currency mix of portfolios would not affect the firm's income, net worth or market value; neither would changes in exchange rates. Thus a central question is whether the deviations from Fisher Open are so large that the concept has little empirical usefulness, or whether, if it is useful, deviations are systematic and predictable or random.

Most international investors act as if they believe the deviations are not random. Typically, U.S. firms prefer to finance their foreign investments by borrowing abroad; the implication is that any additional interest payments are small relative to the probable depreciation of the foreign currencies relative to the dollar. The validity of this proposition seems questionable on an *a priori* basis, since it implies that lenders who hold assets denominated in foreign currencies incur systematic losses because interest rates on these assets are low relative to the rates at which these currencies are depreciating. Indeed, if investors demand a premium for bearing exchange risk and believe the risks greater on assets denominated in the weaker currencies, then in the long run offshore financing may be more expensive than dollar financing after adjustment for changes in exchange rates.

Fisher Open can be examined for both long-term securities and for short-term securities — and for a continuing sequence of short-term investments. Fisher Open can be examined using the interest agio, $r_f - r_d$, and the exchange agio, $(F_t - S_t)/S_t$, as predictions of the rate of change in the exchange rate, $\dot{e}^*/e$. Alternatively, the forward exchange rate, F_t, can be viewed as a prediction of the spot exchange rate, S_{t+n}, at the maturity of the forward contract. Systematic differences between $r_f - r_d$ and $\grave{e}^*/e$, between $(F_t - S_t)/S_t$ and $\grave{e}^*/e$, or between F_t and S_{t+n}, suggest an unexploited profit opportunity. The statement that Fisher Open holds implies that the deviations of the observed values of exchange rates from the predicted values are not significant. The maximum deviation from Fisher Open that might be deemed insignificant must be determined.

If investors believe that domestic and foreign securities are identical in terms of political risk, then the deviations from Fisher Open based on the interest agio and on the exchange agio should not differ. Since in fact the securities issued in the several countries and denominated in the host-country currencies differ in terms of political risk, systematic differences between the exchange rates predicted from the interest agios and the observed exchange rates may represent a payment associated with political risk rather than unexploited profit opportunities.

If there are systematic deviations from Fisher Open, then it would seem that investors have not taken advantage of profit opportunities, perhaps because of transactions costs, exchange controls or the anticipation of such controls, or some other deterrent to arbitrage. Deviations between the predicted exchange rates and the observed exchange rates may be random or systematic. Deviations reflect that the future is uncertain. At any moment, investors' views of the future exchange rates reflect their evaluation of the impacts of current and anticipated monetary policies on the price levels and on exchange rates. The information available to investors changes continuously. Some new information leads investors to reduce their estimates of the rates at which particular currencies will appreciate or depreciate; other information leads them to increase their estimates.

Examining Fisher Open encounters the problem that comparable interest rate data are available for only about ten countries, especially for an extended period. Moreover, while Treasury Bills in one country appear similar to Treasury Bills in other countries, they are imperfect substitutes in terms of susceptibility to default risk.

The first section of this chapter examines long-term interest rate data to determine whether there are systematic deviations between the predictions of the exchange rates and the observed exchange rates. The second section examines the predictive power of the short-term interest agios and of the exchange agio. The predictive power of both agios about the time of parity changes is then examined. The basic questions are whether the empirical data are inconsistent with Fisher Open, and whether there are systematic errors in the predictions, which would suggest an unexploited profit opportunity.

The data examined in this chapter involve observations with the pegged rate system in the late 1960s and early 1970s, and with the floating rate system since then; more observations are available for the pegged rate period. Two *a priori* arguments about the magnitude of the deviations from Fisher Open under the floating and pegged exchange rates are relevant: one is that the deviations might be somewhat smaller under the pegged rate system because central bank intervention in the exchange market is intended to reduce uncertainty about future exchange rates; the other is that deviations might be larger under the pegged rate system, especially in anticipation of changes in the parities, because the parities are changed only with great delay.

FISHER OPEN AND LONG-TERM GOVERNMENT SECURITIES

Fisher Open can be examined by comparing the rates of return from holding long-term dollar securities with the rates of return from holding comparable long-term securities denominated in various foreign currencies. The test of Fisher Open is whether the rates of return on dollar and on the foreign securities differ significantly, after adjustment for changes in the exchange rates and for any other differences in the U.S. and foreign securities.[1]

Throughout the post-war period, interest rates on government securities in most foreign countries were generally higher than interest rates on U.S. government securities. One exception is that interest rates on securities denominated in the Swiss franc were below those on dollar securities, which reflects the tax and other advantages associated with Swiss securities. The Swiss capital market generally has been open to foreign lenders and depositors while foreigners have been subject to limits on the amounts they can borrow in Switzerland.

Table 6.1 compares the compound rates of return for five different holding periods from owning long-term U.S. government bonds and comparable long-term bonds issued by various foreign governments and denominated in their currencies. The premise in the table is that an investor acquired $1 million of U.S. bonds at the beginning of one of the holding periods and the equivalent, at the base period exchange rates, of $1 million in bonds denominated in each of the foreign currencies at the same time; the investments in the U.S. and in the foreign bonds were compounded annually at the applicable long-term interest rate for each year. Then the accumulated foreign values are converted into dollars at

TABLE 6.1 Tests of Fisher Open: Long-Term Government Bonds
(annual average rates of return)

Terminal year	Initial year									
	1950	1955	1960	1965	1970	1950	1955	1960	1965	1970
				UNITED STATES						
1955	3.17									
1960	3.39	4.18								
1965	3.61	4.11	4.87							
1970	4.07	4.57	5.18	6.36						
1975	4.52	5.01	5.56	6.35	7.69					
				CANADA						
1955	5.19					2.02				
1960	4.83	5.13				1.44	0.95			
1965	4.40	4.33	4.59			0.79	0.22	0.28		
1970	5.31	5.57	6.32	9.19		1.24	1.00	1.14	2.83	
1975	5.81	6.13	6.82	8.50	9.47	1.29	1.12	1.26	2.15	1.78
				GREAT BRITAIN						
1955	4.59					1.42				
1960	5.00	6.31				1.61	2.13			
1965	5.34	6.17	7.22			1.73	2.06	2.35		
1970	5.14	5.63	5.87	5.89		1.07	1.06	0.69	−0.47	
1975	5.67	6.17	6.52	6.85	9.74	1.15	1.16	0.96	0.50	2.05
				BELGIUM						
1955	5.72					2.55				
1960	5.58	6.40				2.19	2.22			
1965	5.66	6.11	6.95			2.05	2.00	2.08		
1970	5.98	6.40	6.96	8.30		1.91	1.83	1.74	1.94	
1975	7.32	7.97	8.88	10.54	14.55	2.80	2.96	3.32	4.19	6.86
				FRANCE						
1955	6.96					3.79				
1960	2.70	−0.38				−0.69	−4.56			
1965	3.49	2.31	6.15			−0.12	−1.80	1.28		
1970	3.62	2.88	5.07	5.09		−0.45	−1.69	−0.11	−1.27	
1975	5.48	5.38	7.74	9.11	15.03	0.96	0.37	2.18	2.75	7.34
				GERMANY						
1955										
1960										
1965	n.a.	n.a.	8.44			n.a.	n.a.	3.57		
1970	n.a.	n.a.	8.90	10.88		n.a.	n.a.	3.72	4.52	
1975	n.a.	n.a.	11.30	13.53	18.11	n.a.	n.a.	5.74	7.18	10.42
				SWITZERLAND						
1955	3.35					0.18				
1960	3.24	3.73				−0.15	−0.45			
1965	3.29	3.56	4.02			−0.32	−0.45	−0.85		
1970	3.66	3.97	4.40	5.59		−0.41	−0.60	−0.78	−0.77	
1975	6.20	7.08	8.44	11.15	18.33	1.68	2.07	2.78	4.80	10.64

TABLE 6.1 (*continued*)

Terminal year	\\ 1950	\\ 1955	\\ 1960	\\ 1965	Initial year \\ 1970	\\ 1950	\\ 1955	\\ 1960	\\ 1965	\\ 1970
				ITALY						
1955	7.25					4.08				
1960	6.79	7.62				3.40	3.44			
1965	6.57	6.88	7.18			2.96	2.77	2.31		
1970	6.73	6.98	7.19	8.64		2.67	2.41	2.01	2.28	
1975	6.77	6.97	7.10	7.78	8.78	2.25	1.96	1.54	1.93	1.09
				NETHERLANDS						
1955	4.07					0.90				
1960	4.31	5.21				0.92	1.03			
1965	4.69	5.33	6.33			1.08	1.22	1.46		
1970	5.28	5.91	6.70	8.23		1.21	1.34	1.52	1.87	
1975	7.06	7.99	9.23	11.31	16.29	2.54	2.98	3.67	4.96	8.60
				SWEDEN						
1955	3.98					0.81				
1960	4.18	5.14				0.79	0.96			
1965	4.59	5.27	6.48			0.98	1.16	1.61		
1970	5.11	5.75	6.59	7.99		1.04	1.18	1.14	1.63	
1975	6.32	7.10	8.13	9.62	12.86	1.80	2.09	2.57	3.27	5.19

Source: *International Financial Statistics.*

the end of the holding period, using the prevailing exchange rates.

The choice of base years and terminal years is important in estimating Fisher Open for long-term securities, both because of the 1949 devaluations of the currencies of other industrial countries by 30 per cent or more and the appreciations of various European currencies and the Japanese yen in the 1970s. Using 1948 rather than 1950 as the base year reduces the dollar equivalent of the rates of return from holding foreign bonds, because of the exchange losses resulting from the 1949 devaluation. Similarly, if 1974 is the terminal year rather than 1972 or 1970, the results change, both because of the higher interest rates on bonds denominated in the European currencies than in the dollar and because of the appreciation of European currencies.

The average annual interest rates on U.S. dollar bonds and on comparable bonds issued in various foreign countries and denominated in their currencies for intervals in multiples of five years are shown in the triangles on the left-hand panel in Table 6.1; the interest rates on the foreign bonds include adjustments for changes in the price of the dollar in terms of the relevant foreign currency. The triangles on the right show the differences between the rates of return on the dollar bonds and on the foreign bonds after adjustment for changes in exchange rates.

The more or less continuous increases in U.S. interest rates are evident from the data for the successive five-year intervals on the northwest/southeast diagonal in the top triangle on the left; interest rates in the most recent five-year period were more than twice as high as those for the first five-year period. Similar patterns of more or less continuous increases adjusted for changes in exchange rates are evident in most other currencies. The sharp increase in interest rates in the most recent period is consistent with Fisher Closed, and the inflation of the 1970s.

For nearly all five-year intervals the rates of return on the various foreign bonds were positive after adjustment for changes in exchange rates; the exception was that of France during the 1955–60 period, when the devaluation of the franc was larger in percentage terms than the excess of the interest rates on franc bonds over the interest rate on dollar bonds.

The rates of return on investments in the Swiss franc bonds were generally below the rates of return on dollar bonds as long as the Swiss franc remained pegged to the dollar for Swiss interest rates were less than U.S. interest rates. With the floating of the franc and its subsequent appreciation, the returns on the Swiss franc bonds exceed those on the dollar bonds; the appreciation is sufficient to dominate the excess of U.S. interest rates over the Swiss interest rates. The difference between the rates of return on the dollar bond and the Swiss franc bond averages to less than 2 per cent a year over a twenty-five-year interval, although the difference is more than 10 per cent a year over the most recent five-year interval.[2]

The rates of return on the Canadian dollar bonds averaged about 1 per cent a year higher than the rates of return on the U.S. bonds.[3] When the Canadian dollar appreciated, as in the 1950–5 period, and again in the 1965–70 period, the excess of the return on the Canadian dollar investment relative to the return on the U.S. dollar investment was unusually high. When the Canadian dollar depreciated sharply, as in 1962, the excess of the return on Canadian securities fell sharply.

For the nine foreign bonds as a group, the rate of return averaged 1.80 per cent higher per year than the rate of return on dollar bonds for the inclusive period. For the most recent five-year period, however, the rate of return on the foreign bonds exceeded that on dollar bonds by more than 6 per cent a year, largely because of the sharp appreciations of the mark and the mark-zone currencies.

For most periods, the rates of return from holding the foreign bonds, with the exception of the Swiss franc bonds, were higher than the rates of return from holding dollar bonds, regardless of whether the foreign currency depreciated or appreciated. Sterling depreciated, yet the rates of return on sterling bonds averaged more than 1 per cent higher than on dollar bonds after adjustment for changes in exchange rates. The Belgian franc, the Dutch guilder and the Swedish krona also appreciated; the rates of return on the bonds denominated in these currencies averaged more than 2 per cent more than those on dollar bonds, partly from their appreciation but largely from the higher interest rates. The implication is that even if investors anticipate that exchange rates will not change, bonds denominated in currencies other than the U.S. dollar are priced to yield 1–2 per cent more a year than U.S. bonds, perhaps because of political risk or because of differential default risk. If a foreign currency depreciates sharply for a brief period, the excess of rates of return on foreign bonds over the rates of return on dollar bonds may decline below this long-run differential.[4]

FISHER OPEN AND SHORT-TERM SECURITIES

Fisher Open can be tested for three different types of short-term securities – forward contracts, Euro-currency deposits. Treasury Bills and prime loans. Since both Treasury Bills and perhaps even prime loans are subject to political risk as well as exchange risk, it seems likely that deviations from Fisher Open would be smallest with forward contracts. Moreover, it seems plausible that the deviations from Fisher Open based on short-term securities would be smaller than those based on long-term securities, since yield curves in most foreign countries are more positively sloped than the yield curve in the United States.

Several questions about Fisher Open can be distinguished. One is whether the forecasts of the future spot rates implicit both in the interest agios for treasury bills and prime loans and in the forward exchange rates are on average biased or unbiased predictors; the question is whether the mean of the predicted rates and the mean of the observed rates on the dates when the predictions mature differ in any significant statistical sense. The second question is which of the several predictors of the future spot exchange rates performs best; in addition to the interest agio and the forward rate, today's spot rate might be considered a predictior of future spot rates. The third question is whether the errors

TABLE 6.2 Deviation from Fisher Open: Short-Term Securities

		1967	1968	1969	1970	1971	1972	1973	1974	1975	1976
CANADA	Treasury Bills										
	M	-0.16	-1.50	-0.77	-6.27	-0.19	0.37	-0.94	2.69	-3.00	1.84
	SD	2.61	2.10	1.19	6.87	3.77	4.92	5.07	4.49	8.50	9.62
	N	52	52	52	52	52	52	52	52	52	52
	Prime loans										
	M	-0.17	-1.26	-0.28	-6.72	-1.55	-0.77	-1.89	2.77	-2.78	2.30
	SD	2.44	1.86	1.09	6.78	3.90	4.78	4.68	4.94	8.35	9.58
	N	52	52	52	52	52	52	52	52	52	52
	Euro-deposits										
	M	0.19	-1.07	0.36	-5.88	-0.04	-0.36	-1.02	3.18	-2.25	1.97
	SD	2.35	1.70	1.19	6.71	3.81	4.87	5.44	4.82	8.89	9.77
	N	52	51	51	52	51	51	52	52	52	52
GREAT BRITAIN	Treasury Bills										
	M	12.52	-1.07	-1.49	-1.41	-8.98	3.57	3.18	-6.82	16.05	5.79
	SD	23.39	1.31	1.06	3.09	5.24	17.24	18.78	12.78	11.66	22.97
	N	52	51	52	52	52	50	52	52	52	52
	Prime loans										
	M	12.85	-0.92	-1.09	-0.90	-8.91	4.19	3.16	-5.74	16.96	6.71
	SD	23.35	1.26	1.15	2.89	5.54	17.24	18.84	13.21	11.31	22.77
	N	52	52	52	52	52	52	52	52	52	52
	Euro-deposits										
	M	13.72	-2.72	-3.52	-1.10	-8.13	3.83	3.04	-7.72	16.25	4.97
	SD	23.50	2.08	2.77	2.79	5.01	17.48	18.95	14.34	11.34	23.29
	N	50	50	51	52	51	51	50	52	52	52
BELGIUM	Treasury Bills										
	M	-1.18	2.40	-1.29	-1.86	-13.31	-8.46	-0.84	-18.31	10.16	-11.48
	SD	1.28	1.57	2.27	0.47	9.74	17.71	32.33	19.38	15.23	12.14
	N	49	52	50	52	52	52	52	52	52	52

TABLE 6.2 *(continued)*

		1967	1968	1969	1970	1971	1972	1973	1974	1975	1976
	Prime loans	M	-1.11	1.39	-1.31	-1.72	-14.54	-8.93	-0.60	-16.58	9.19	-10.42
		SD	1.05	1.58	-2.38	0.45	-10.08	17.84	32.77	19.99	14.82	12.22
		N	52	52	52	52	52	52	52	52	52	51
	Euro-deposits	M	-0.14	2.59	-1.96	0.15	-11.29	-8.80	0.52	-16.27	11.58	-12.18
		SD	1.14	1.71	4.28	0.50	9.82	18.72	32.45	20.08	15.43	12.20
		N	48	48	45	49	49	48	52	52	52	52
FRANCE	Treasury Bills	M	n.a.	n.a.	n.a.	-2.37	-11.11	-10.93	3.17	n.a.	13.16	4.62
		SD	n.a.	n.a.	n.a.	0.43	13.51	20.11	35.15	n.a.	13.36	9.90
		N	n.a.	n.a.	n.a.	35	52	52	52	n.a.	40	50
	Prime loans	M	-1.29	0.48	9.60	-2.59	-12.18	-12.27	2.85	-17.70	3.51	4.06
		SD	1.78	2.12	19.45	0.66	13.61	19.92	33.19	14.26	18.51	9.10
		N	52	52	52	52	52	52	52	51	52	52
	Euro-deposits	M	-0.05	-0.06	4.53	-1.14	-6.07	-9.85	5.24	-20.30	5.48	2.93
		SD	-2.03	4.64	16.88	0.54	12.12	20.75	36.65	14.29	18.69	9.64
		N	51	24	37	52	49	51	52	52	52	52
GERMANY	Treasury Bills	M	1.46	3.11	-6.96	-1.45	-14.44	-9.47	-10.21	-13.09	13.50	-5.30
		SD	1.45	3.05	12.87	1.71	4.67	21.62	42.83	24.65	15.25	9.88
		N	52	—	52	51	52	52	52	52	43	52
	Prime loans	M	-0.29	0.93	-8.71	-3.15	-15.86	-11.75	-13.28	-15.02	7.94	-7.69
		SD	1.71	2.88	12.57	1.61	4.85	21.75	42.78	24.73	15.79	9.87
		N	52	52	52	52	52	52	52	52	52	52
	Euro-deposits	M	1.45	3.46	-6.03	-1.04	-12.52	-8.25	-5.13	-11.66	10.87	-5.72
		SD	1.45	3.16	12.09	2.11	5.13	22.13	44.27	25.36	16.14	10.11
		N	52	51	51	52	52	51	46	52	52	52

TABLE 6.2 *(continued)*

		1967	1968	1969	1970	1971	1972	1973	1974	1975	1976
ITALY											
Treasury Bills	M	n.a.	n.a.	n.a.	-2.24	-8.65	-3.47	11.34	-3.78	8.12	-5.44
	SD	n.a.	n.a.	n.a.	1.46	5.91	6.07	21.67	11.39	12.55	10.27
	N	n.a.	n.a.	n.a.	35	52	52	52	52	40	40
Prime loans	M	-1.77	-0.21	1.39	-2.83	-9.69	-4.27	10.76	-5.42	17.17	-1.59
	SD	0.91	1.87	1.30	1.94	5.81	6.09	20.95	13.94	29.58	18.66
	N	52	52	52	52	52	52	52	52	52	52
Euro-deposits	M	0.34	1.09	0.57	-3.27	-5.68	-2.40	11.04	-9.49	18.38	-6.79
	SD	0.94	1.12	2.06	4.29	5.73	6.31	20.42	12.46	29.67	21.88
	N	40	42	39	48	43	50	47	52	50	49
NETHERLANDS											
Treasury Bills	M	-0.28	1.04	0.34	-1.13	(-5.03)	-6.97	-3.08	-16.47	(1.65)	—
	SD	1.45	1.82	2.85	1.09	(4.96)	19.21	32.48	17.51	(5.25)	—
	N	52	45	46	52	(7)	52	52	51	(15)	
Prime loans	M	-0.86	0.65	0.75	-1.93	-14.15	-8.90	-6.56	-15.54	9.90	-8.49
	SD	1.21	1.79	2.42	1.18	7.61	18.77	31.87	18.28	13.89	13.18
	N	52	52	52	52	52	52	52	52	52	52
Euro-deposits	M	0.28	1.73	1.63	-0.32	-10.58	-5.99	-4.67	-14.11	12.19	-9.06
	SD	1.63	1.84	3.14	1.17	7.56	19.86	30.81	18.48	15.10	15.49
	N	52	51	51	52	50	51	51	52	52	52

TABLE 6.2 (*continued*)

		1967	1968	1969	1970	1971	1972	1973	1974	1975	1976
SWITZERLAND Prime loans	M	0.04	-0.19	1.26	0.49	-12.42	-18.32	-4.92	-20.91	1.93	-2.30
	SD	1.47	1.90	1.60	2.20	6.29	25.81	32.64	24.79	15.36	9.85
	N	52	52	52	52	52	52	52	52	52	51
Euro-deposits	M	1.11	1.28	1.32	1.17	-7.74	-14.43	-2.72	-22.72	5.05	2.69
	SD	1.69	1.47	1.52	1.55	7.61	27.35	32.72	25.13	14.88	9.75
	N	52	51	51	52	52	51	52	52	52	52

M = Mean deviation; SD = standard deviation; N = no. of deviations.

in the predictions of successive spot rates are random or whether instead forecast errors are systematically related, which would indicate that there is a persistent bias in the forecast.

The results of the tests of Fisher Open for these three types of securities for eight countries are shown in Table 6.2 for each year in the 1967–76 decade.[5] The first few years in the sample period (1967–70) are towards the end of the pegged rate period, while the last few years (1973–6) are part of the floating rate period. Comparisons can be made among these three securities as well as across periods. A positive entry indicates that the currency appreciated by less or depreciated by more than the forecast.

The deviations from Fisher Open in the floating rate period are generally larger than in the pegged rate period, and in some cases by a substantial amount; these deviations reflect the increase in uncertainty in the monetary environment. Year-to-year variations in the deviations during the floating rate period have been substantial; however, they may be declining. The variance of the forecast errors is substantially larger during the floating rate system, and increased by a larger amount than the mean forecast errors increased, indicating that 'forecasting' is more difficult under the floating rate system.

The Euro-currency interest rates appear to be better predictors of the future spot exchange rates than either of the other two interest agios, both during the floating rate period and during the pegged rate period, especially for the more volatile currencies. The data suggest that the interest agios based on Treasury Bills may perform somewhat better as a predictor of future spot exchange rates than agios based on prime loans.

None of the 'forecast errors' is statistically significant for the various currencies. The implication is that the various predictions of the future spot rate are unbiased – or at least the hypothesis that the forecasts are unbiased cannot be denied.[6]

An infinite number of comparisons might be made about the effectiveness of competing approaches towards predicting future spot exchange rates. In addition to using forward rates and the interest agios to predict future spot rates, today's spot rates might be used to predict future spot rates. A prediction about future spot rates might be based on changes in the money supply – money demand relationship in the several countries. The forecasts of future spot rates might be derived from large econometric models which include changes in the balance of payments or the trade balances along with changes in money supplies and relative prices as explanatory variables. A time-series model might be used to generate the estimates of the future spot rate, based on the past history of the exchange rate movements. The information in several of these forecasts might be combined into a composite forecast.

The general conclusion from such comparisons is that the Euro-currency rates or the forward exchange rates are the best predictors of future spot exchange rates. The forward rate underpredicts most sharp changes in the spot exchange rates, but so do all other forecasts.[7] One reason why the forward rates perform so well is that they are continuously updated on an hour-to-hour, day-to-day basis; the investors who seek to change their exposure are likely to do so by undertaking one or more forward transactions, as long as the forward rate differs from the anticipated spot rate. Consequently, the forward rates incorporate most of the information about future spot rates that is already in the market – the information that might lead investors to revise their estimates of future spot rates may lead them to undertake forward transactions.

The third question is whether the errors between the predicted spot exchange rates and the spot exchange rates on the data when the predictions mature are random or systematic. Systematic errors suggest an unexploited profit opportunity. The pattern of period-to-period movements in exchange rates was examined for systematic movements, to determine whether there are 'runs' in the rate movements, or whether the exchange rates follow a random walk. If there are runs, investors might devise trading rules in the anticipation that persistent profits could be realised by identifying and following the trends. Profits would be attainable even though forward rates might, on average, be effective predictors of the future spot exchange rates. In contrast, if the exchange rate movements do not differ significantly from a random walk, then it should not be possible to develop trading rules which lead to systematic profits.

The results of tests for autocorrelations of the residuals between predicted exchange rates and observed exchange rates for seven countries are shown in Table 6.3. The reversal of signs as the length of the lags is increased, and the small values of the coefficients, are consistent with the view that the errors in the forecasts are not systematically related.[8]

FISHER OPEN AND CHANGES IN PARITIES

Under the pegged exchange rate system, changes in parities are sudden; within a day or so, the exchange parity might change by 15 or 20 per

TABLE 6.3 Tests of Autocorrelations of Residuals of Forecasts

	Lags	Prime rates	Forward rates	Treasury Bills
CANADA	1	0.36	0.38	0.36
	2	−0.12	−0.14	−0.13
	3	−0.38	−0.39	−0.38
	4	−0.50	−0.50	−0.48
	5	−0.36	−0.35	−0.33
GREAT BRITAIN	1	−0.16	−0.13	−0.15
	2	−0.08	−0.08	−0.08
	3	0.10	0.09	0.08
	4	−0.01	−0.02	−0.02
	5	−0.29	−0.31	−0.30
BELGIUM	1	−0.15	−0.09	−0.10
	2	−0.37	−0.32	−0.36
	3	0.19	0.14	0.15
	4	−0.19	−0.24	−0.21
	5	−0.32	−0.34	−0.34
FRANCE	1	0.11	0.15	−
	2	−0.29	−0.25	−
	3	−0.07	−0.10	−
	4	−0.25	−0.27	−
	5	−0.31	−0.34	−
GERMANY	1	−0.25	−0.26	−0.24
	2	−0.33	−0.35	−0.33
	3	0.31	0.32	0.26
	4	−0.18	−0.18	−0.21
	5	−0.17	−0.19	−0.10
NETHERLANDS	1	−0.17	−0.15	−
	2	−0.32	−0.28	−
	3	0.25	0.23	−
	4	−0.20	−0.21	−
	5	−0.20	−0.31	−
SWITZERLAND	1	−0.20	−0.4	−
	2	−0.34	−0.31	−
	3	0.11	0.13	−
	4	−0.19	−0.19	−
	5	−0.09	−0.12	−

cent, or even more. While few such changes are totally unexpected, their timing is frequently a surprise. The more completely such changes are anticipated, the greater the opportunity that investors have to profit at the expense of the monetary authorities. The stronger the anticipation of such changes, the more likely they may be reflected in the interest rate

TABLE 6.4 Predicted and Observed Parity Changes
(in annual percentage rates)

		$t-12$	$t-6$	$t-3$	$t-2$	$t-1$	t_0	$t+1$	$t+2$	$t+3$
British sterling:										
1967	Interest agio	1.75	1.44	1.20	1.50	0.87	16.7	1.03	2.16	1.66
	Exchange agio	1.08	0.06	-0.17	-0.09	0.06		-0.38	0.49	0.08
1971	Interest agio	0.44	2.80	1.51	0.91	0.27	F	0.17	0.14	0.10
	Exchange agio	1.00	2.50	0.77	0.48	2.34		-2.00	-2.50	-1.28
1972	Interest agio	Pre-pegging		2.84	1.60	1.42	F	0.31	-3.13	-2.36
	Exchange agio			2.27	0.73	0.30		0.00	-3.76	-3.29
Belgian franc:										
1971	Interest agio	1.25	2.11	1.76	0.84	2.70	11.6	1.74	5.67	5.54
	Exchange agio	-0.16	0.20	0.28	-0.14	2.07		4.11	5.58	5.11
French franc:										
1969	Interest agio	1.16	3.54	1.18	1.77	2.10	12.3	1.21	2.39	2.80
	Exchange agio	0.44	0.26	-0.38	-0.14	0.22		-0.79	0.11	0.68
1971	Interest agio	1.86	1.94	1.70	2.03	1.40	F	-0.1	0.61	6.78
	Exchange agio	0.04	0.25	0.16	0.01	0.22		4.00	5.96	7.16
German mark:										
1969	Interest agio	-3.28	-2.28	-2.90	-1.45	-0.59	8.5	-1.07	-1.27	-1.02
	Exchange agio	-1.41	-0.13	-2.11	-1.09	-0.48		-0.49	-0.21	0.38
1971	Interest agio	0.33	0.15	1.42	1.25	4.29	F	4.74	2.54	1.82
	Exchange agio	0.03	-0.47	0.28	0.22	2.66		5.20	3.30	1.37

TABLE 6.4 (*Continued*)

		$t-12$	$t-6$	$t-3$	$t-2$	$t-1$	t_0	$t+1$	$t+2$	$t+3$
Duch guilder:										
1971	Interest agio	−0.17	1.06	1.97	0.99	3.03	F	2.97	3.18	4.76
	Exchange agio	−0.11	0.08	0.58	0.84	2.60		7.76	9.26	4.66
Swiss franc:										
1971	Interest agio	−3.52	−3.72	−2.03	−0.09	−0.90	F	−0.16	−0.47	−0.35
	Exchange agio	0.00	−0.70	−0.02	0.21	0.07		2.22	3.21	1.89
Canadian dollar:										
1970	Interest agio	0.67	1.13	0.08	−0.13	3.55	F	0.66	0.67	0.66
	Exchange agio	−0.19	0.41	0.03	0.09	−0.08		1.16	.43	−0.14

F = move to a floating rate.

differential and the forward exchange rate prior to the change in the parity. At times, statements are made that the forward discount is so large that profits cannot be made by selling the currency forward. Table 6.4 indicates the magnitudes of the interest agios and the exchange agios in the months prior to changes in parities and subsequent to these changes. The percentage change in the parity is shown in the column headed t_0; an F indicates the country moved from a pegged to a floating rate system. The values for the interest agio and the exchange agio in the months prior to the parity change are indicated in the columns $t - 1$, $t - 2$, etc.; the integer refers to the number of months before or after the change in the parity occurred. Both the interest agios and the exchange agios greatly understate the amount of the changes in the parity. There is little evidence that the size of the agios increases as the date of the changes in the parity approaches, and there is no evidence that the forward discount becomes so large that the profits from selling the currency forward in anticipation of the change in the exchange rate are no longer feasible.[9]

SUMMARY

The examination of the deviations from Fisher Open using long-term securities shows that most of the deviations from Fisher Open are smaller than 2 per cent a year. The deviations for a sequence of investment in short-term securities are smaller than the deviations for long-term securities, and the deviations using forward exchange rates are generally smaller than those derived from the interest rate data. When exchange parities change, the deviations from Fisher Open are very large, both when the interest rates and forward exchange rates are used; the deviations do not appear to decline in the intervals prior to the changes in parities.

The deviations from Fisher Open are of about the same magnitude as the deviations from Purchasing Power Parity, both on an aggregative basis and, where the data permit, on a country-by-country basis.

7. Interest Rate Differentials and Political Risk

Political risk is customarily associated with the expropriation of local branches of foreign firms by the host-country governments, usually with inadequate compensation, mostly within developing countries. Consequently, many firms prefer to borrow locally to finance their foreign subsidiaries to minimise their exposure to losses from expropriation; they anticipate that if a subsidiary is expropriated, its new owners would be obliged to repay its debts, and the parent firm would be free of any remaining financial obligation. A second, less dramatic concern with political risk involves changes in exchange controls – firms are concerned about host-country constraints on the payment of dividends and the repayment of capital;[1] they want to 'get their money out' as soon as possible.

Both concerns – expropriation and exchange controls – lead foreign firms to borrow as much as possible within the host countries. As a consequence, interest rates within these countries may be somewhat higher than the amount that can be attributed solely to anticipated changes in exchange rates.

The analogy with exchange risk suggests it would be useful to compare the accumulated value of that component of the interest rate differential that might be attributed to political risk with the losses when investments are expropriated, or when exchange controls are applied or become more restrictive. The calculation is complex, and for several reasons. The first is the ambiguity about the amount that investors spend to avoid or reduce their exposure to political risk; this amount is not measurable directly, but must be obtained by decomposing the interest agio into a payment for exchange risk and a payment for political risk. The second is that the losses attributable to expropriation and changes in exchange controls are not nearly as unambiguous as the losses and gains from changes in exchange rates, for such controls may discriminate among investors by the nature of the assets they own, and even by the country in which they are domiciled.[2] Hence the comparisons between the costs incurred to avoid the losses due to expropriation and exchange controls and the amount of these losses when subsidiaries are taken over or exchange controls raised can only be approximate.

The cases of expropriation have been extensively documented.[3] In the immediate aftermath of the Second World War foreign investors lost properties in Eastern Europe with the rearrangement of borders and governments. Castro in Cuba, Sukarno in Indonesia, Nkrumah in Ghana, and Allende in Chile took over the properites of foreign firms. Newly independent countries have taken over properties owned by firms based in the metropolitan country; thus the properties of Dutch firms in Indonesia, French firms in Algeria and Vietnam, and British firms in East Africa were expropriated. Various petroleum companies were obliged to sell their producing properties to the host-country governments, sometimes at book value, or at least at prices substantially below the market value of the earning power of the assets. The aggregate losses for firms in all industries other than petroleum are probably in the order of several billions of dollars for all of the 1950–75 period, and the inclusion of firms in the extractive industries raises the total modestly.

These losses over a twenty-five-year period can be compared with the additional interest costs because firms borrowed within the host countries rather than in the United States. If this additional interest cost is 1 per cent a year and the borrowing in host countries averaged $100 billion, annual losses due to expropriation would have to exceed $1 billion before borrowing abroad would appear justifiable in economic terms alone. This comparison is downward-biased in that the interest rate differential attributable to political risk is greater than 1 per cent, while the amount of host-country borrowing has exceeded $100 billion. The implication is that the losses attributable to expropriation and exchange controls have been smaller than the costs incurred to avoid such losses.[4]

This chapter examines two measurable aspects of the political risk premia attached to short-term financial assets. One involves deviations from Interest Rate Parity, and the second involves deviations between onshore and offshore interest rates. In the first, exchange risk has been fully hedged; in the second, onshore and offshore interest rates involve assets denominated in the same currency, so again there is no exchange risk. In both cases the interest rate differentials reflect either actual or anticipated barriers to arbitrage across national borders. The central question is whether – *ex post* – the additional interest payment to avoid political risk premia are large relative to the losses that investors incur.

DEVIATIONS FROM INTEREST RATE PARITY

If assets issued in different countries are not deemed significantly different in terms of susceptibility to political risk, the interest agio and the exchange agio would not differ by more than transactions costs.[5] Deviations smaller than those attributable to transactions costs would be random. Larger deviations would either represent some other systematic factor, such as exchange controls or taxes on international capital flows, or the anticipation that exchange controls might be raised before funds can be repatriated from offshore centres. To the extent investors believe that assets issued in various centres differ in terms of political risk, there may be persistent differences between the interest agio and the exchange agio. How long such anticipations deter arbitrage remains an empirical question.

The data needed to calculate deviations from Interest Rate Parity are the time series of money market interest rates and of forward exchange rates for comparable maturities. Moreover, the money market securities in the several countries should be similar in terms of the sensitivity to default risk; the securities sold by branches of the same financial institution in several countries would be preferable to the securities of the host-country governments. Taxes on interest income in the several countries should not differ significantly.

The average annual deviations from Interest Rate Parity for nine countries relative to the United States for each year in the decade 1967–76 are shown in Table 7.1.[6] Deviations from Interest Rate Parity are shown based on prime commercial loans (no adjustment is made for differences among countries in the levels of compensating balances) as well as on Treasury Bills. When securities are identical in terms of exchange risk, the deviations in excess of 0.25 per cent would be relatively unusual; smaller deviations might be considered insignificant. Negative deviations mean that the discount on the foreign currency in the forward market exceeds the excess of foreign interest rates over U.S. interest rates; exchange controls deter investors resident within the foreign countries from selling these currencies spot and buying them forward. Negative deviations generally are associated with weak currencies and reflect barriers to outward arbitrage; positive deviations are associated with strong currencies and reflect barriers to inward arbitrage.

The deviations for Germany, Switzerland and the Netherlands frequently exceeded 2 per cent. Investors not resident in these countries were constrained from buying their currencies spot and selling them

TABLE 7.1 Average Annual Deviations from Interest Rate Parity

	1967	1968	1969	1970	1971	1972	1973	1974	1975	1976
CANADA										
Treasury Bills	−0.21	−0.32	1.04	0.22	−0.10	−0.80	−0.10	0.29	0.53	−0.37
Prime loans	−0.14	−0.57	0.52	0.62	1.21	0.32	0.90	0.27	0.36	−0.89
GREAT BRITAIN										
Treasury Bills	0.43	−1.97	−2.67	0.03	0.66	−0.18	−1.42	−2.01	−0.60	−2.01
Prime loans	0.09	−2.17	−3.14	−0.34	0.55	−0.51	−1.34	−3.01	−1.55	−2.98
BELGIUM										
Treasury Bills	0.86	−0.11	−1.54	1.67	2.11	0.90	2.44	−0.81	0.50	−2.60
Prime loans	0.77	0.88	−1.88	1.59	3.29	1.37	2.30	−2.45	1.31	−3.70
FRANCE										
Treasury Bills	n.a.	n.a.	n.a.	1.02	3.99	1.25	1.67	n.a.	−0.18	−2.34
Prime loans	1.12	−2.34	−6.88	0.99	5.01	2.61	2.00	−3.97	1.36	−1.89
GERMANY										
Treasury Bills	−0.06	0.24	1.62	0.03	1.71	1.70	2.87	1.22	0.94	−0.34
Prime loans	1.65	2.46	3.39	1.82	3.10	3.83	5.92	3.32	2.91	1.98
ITALY										
Treasury Bills	n.a.	n.a.	n.a.	−0.56	2.39	0.11	−3.08	−8.48	−3.85	11.65
Prime loans	1.83	1.25	−1.26	−2.61	3.51	−0.80	−2.13	−7.56	0.89	−9.17
NETHERLANDS										
Treasury Bills	0.30	0.51	0.40	0.54	2.16	1.26	0.59	2.88	1.55	n.a.
Prime loans	0.84	1.14	0.72	1.49	3.47	3.16	1.45	1.03	2.24	−1.20
SWITZERLAND										
Treasury Bills	n.a.									
Prime loans	0.94	1.58	0.20	0.41	4.24	4.65	2.67	−2.26	2.79	4.67
JAPAN										
Treasury Bills	n.a.									
Prime loans	n.a.	n.a.	n.a.	2.16	6.21	8.87	3.64	−7.33	−0.54	−0.76

n.a. = adequate data not available.
Source: Harris Trust Tape

forward because at times these countries used exchange controls to keep foreign funds out. In Britain and Italy, in contrast, the deviations were usually negative and reflect barriers to the outflow of arbitrage funds. Deviations have been smaller in the Canadian dollar than in any other currency. The deviations for a number of countries, including Switzerland and the Netherlands as well as Britain and Italy, have been larger during the floating rate period than in the pegged rate period. The deviations based on the prime loan data are generally larger than those based on the Treasury Bill data.

The observed deviations from Interest Rate Parity mean that investors have been deterred by exchange controls or by anticipation of such controls from taking advantage of an apparent profit opportunity – which appears at least riskless in terms of changes in exchange rates.[7] No attempt is made to determine the extent of losses (or gains) attributable to changes in exchange controls, although casual observation suggests that the deviations are large relative to such losses. The implication is that firms pay a substantial premium to avoid exposure to political risk, even more than they pay to avoid exposure to exchange risk.

DEVIATIONS BETWEEN ONSHORE AND OFFSHORE INTEREST RATES

That interest rates on offshore deposits exceed those on comparable onshore deposits by more than transactions costs must reflect one of two factors: either exchange controls limit arbitrage from the domestic to offshore centres, or the anticipation of such controls on the repatriation of funds from the 'offshore' country limits the flows to offshore centres. From 1963 to 1973 the U.S. Interest Equalisation Tax and the Voluntary and Mandatory Credit Restraint Programs limited arbitrage by U.S. residents from domestic to offshore centres; at times, offshore dollar interest rates were 3 percentage points higher than on comparable domestic deposits.

The more severe are domestic exchange controls, the higher offshore interest rates may become relative to domestic interest rates. Since the investor contemplating a shift of funds from the onshore market to the offshore market may choose among a range of centres in which to acquire offshore deposits, the major deterrent to arbitrage is likely to be the exchange controls in the domestic country.

Traditionally, offshore interest rates have risen relative to onshore rates during periods of monetary stringency as borrowers who are unable to satisfy their demands for funds in the domestic market sought funds offshore, especially when ceilings were applied to domestic interest rates. Moreover, when interest rates on offshore dollar deposits rose relative to those on domestic dollar deposits, echo effects were observed in the interest rates on offshore deposits denominated in other currencies.[8]

TABLE 7.2 Differentials Between Onshore and Offshore Interest Rates
(Treasury Bills and 90-Day Euro-deposits, per cent per year)

	1967	1968	1969	1970	1971	1972	1973	1974	1975	1976
UNITED STATES										
Mean	−1.19	−1.06	−3.14	−2.25	−2.37	−1.45	−2.35	−3.03	−1.26	−0.62
SD	0.30	0.32	0.98	0.38	0.83	0.44	0.79	1.75	0.56	0.17
CANADA										
Mean	−0.87	−0.58	−1.88	−1.82	−2.28	−2.12	−2.39	−2.69	−0.44	−0.56
SD	0.37	0.75	0.71	0.35	0.64	0.45	0.79	0.67	0.52	0.31
GREAT BRITAIN										
Mean	−0.49	−2.73	−5.75	−2.06	−1.49	−1.42	−3.29	−4.41	−1.24	−0.97
SD	0.32	1.78	3.01	0.64	0.90	0.87	1.26	1.39	1.59	0.78
BELGIUM										
Mean	0.04	−0.86	−3.72	−0.13	−0.26	−0.75	−1.00	−0.91	0.14	−0.73
SD	0.30	0.65	3.25	0.49	0.90	0.67	0.62	1.59	0.58	0.81
FRANCE										
Mean	n.a.	n.a.	n.a.	0.78	1.57	0.07	−0.48	n.a.	−0.99	−2.47
SD	n.a.	n.a.	n.a.	0.63	2.17	0.58	0.91	n.a.	1.28	1.41
GERMANY										
Mean	−1.25	−0.77	−1.64	−2.05	−0.44	0.26	0.79	−1.65	−0.24	−0.52
SD	0.35	0.37	1.24	1.23	0.77	0.95	2.54	1.08	1.13	0.34
ITALY										
Mean	n.a.	n.a.	n.a.	−5.44	0.80	−0.37	−3.47	−9.69	−4.97	−8.68
SD	n.a.	n.a.	n.a.	4.55	5.56	2.83	4.73	4.79	3.83	6.92
NETHERLANDS										
Mean	−0.65	−0.47	−3.17	−1.55	0.58	−0.08	−1.45	0.27	0.37	n.a.
SD	0.25	0.65	1.37	0.69	0.55	0.92	2.06	1.24	1.44	n.a.

The average annual deviations between interest rates on domestic and offshore dollar and non-dollar deposits are shown in Table 7.2 for each year in the last decade. When credit was unusually tight in the United States in 1969 and 1974 the excess of offshore rates over onshore rates was unusually high. Thus the deviation between the two types of dollar deposits reached 3 per cent and was rarely below 1 per cent. Changes in interest rates on offshore dollar deposits were transmitted to interest rates on offshore deposits denominated in other currencies.[9] Thus in 1974 the deviations were large in most currencies. In addition, there is a country or currency effect; the offshore interest rates in currencies other than the dollar were set by the interest rate on Euro-dollars and the forward rate for each currency against the dollar. The spread between offshore and onshore rates was generally more volatile in various foreign currencies than in the dollar. When investors anticipated that certain currencies might be revalued and the authorities in these countries adopted measures to limit the inflows of funds, as Germany and the Netherlands did in the early 1970s, interest rates on offshore deposits denominated in these currencies fell below interest rates on domestic deposits. In contrast, when investors anticipated that a currency might depreciate, and a forward discount appeared on this currency, as was the case for the French franc in 1976 and the Italian lira in 1974, the excess of offshore over onshore interest rates increased sharply.

With the Canadian dollar, offshore interest rates exceeded domestic interest rates by as much as 2 per cent during some years, and by an average of 1.5 per cent for the decade. Offshore interest rates on sterling deposits averaged more than 2.5 per cent more than those on onshore deposits. In contrast, interest rates on offshore mark deposits exceeded those on onshore deposits by an average of less than 1 per cent a year, and in two years of the decade interest rates on onshore deposits were higher.

INTEREST RATE PARITY AND EXTERNAL CURRENCY

The deviations between onshore and offshore interest rates can be compared with the deviations from Interest Rate Parity. Offshore dollar rates always exceed onshore rates, and a similar yield relationship prevails for other currencies most of the time. Whenever the deviation from interest parity is positive because a currency is strong, the offshore interest rate may be below the onshore rate for this currency. Similarly, whenever a currency is weak and at a substantial forward discount, offshore interest rates exceed onshore rates for this currency by an unusually large amount. The premium for political risk inferred from the differential between onshore and offshore interest rates generally exceeds that inferred from Interest Rate Parity. In both cases the differentials frequently exceed 2 per cent.

SUMMARY

The political risk premium can be measured using deviations from

Interest Rate Parity and deviations between onshore and offshore deposits denominated in different currencies. That deviations exceed transactions costs reflects either exchange controls or the anticipations of such controls. Frequently these deviations average more than 2 per cent a year; the deviations using the onshore − offshore interest rates are generally larger than the deviations from Interest Rate Parity.

Part II

Introduction to Part II

The corporate treasurer is primarily concerned with managing the capital structure of the firm and allocating its funds among competing investments. Changes in exchange rates and exchange controls – uncertain events whose timing and magnitude are unknown – affect the returns on various activities of the firm, its borrowing costs, and its income and net worth. Someone must decide whether the firm should hold assets and liabilities denominated in various foreign currencies. This decision involves a comparison of the risk–return trade-off on assets and liabilities denominated in foreign currencies with the risk–return trade-off in the firm's other activities.

The corporate treasurer must deal with four questions. The first involves how the firm's net worth and income would be affected by changes in exchange rates, which entails estimation of the firm's exposure to exchange risk. The second is how the firm can alter its exposure to insulate its net worth and income from changes in exchange rates, and the costs of alternative ways of changing exposure. The third question involves the impact of taxes on the firm's exposure and the techniques used to alter its exposure. The fourth question is whether the firm's interests are served by altering its exposure.

The traditional approach towards these four questions has been eclectic, with a minimal basis in logic and in the data. In contrast, the analysis that underlies the chapters in Part II rests on the systematic relationships discussed in Chapters 3 and 4 and the empirical findings evaluated in Chapters 5, 6 and 7.

The central issue for strategic decisions involves determining the exposure of the firm – how its net worth, or its income, or its market value would be affected by changes in exchange rates and changes in exchange controls. The techniques that a firm might use to alter the currency mix of its assets and liabilities and the costs and returns of changing its exposure are discussed in Chapter 8. The recommendations of accountants and of economists towards estimation of the firm's exposure to exchange risk are discussed in Chapter 9.

The focus of Chapter 10 is on how the corporate tax structure affects the firm's attitudes towards exposure to exchange risk and political risk. If the firm holds assets denominated in foreign currencies, changes in exchange rates may result in capital gains or losses in some circumstances, and in ordinary gains and losses in others. Hence the firm's after-tax income may change as a result of changes in its tax liabilities.

Chapter 11 presents some 'cookbook' strategies that the firm might follow towards the exchange risk problem. These several strategies are appraised in terms of the data discussed in Chapters 5 and 6.

Chapter 12 develops a general strategy towards exchange risk. Uncertainty is recognised more explicitly, and the impact of uncertainty is evaluated.

8. The Costs of Altering Exposure to Exchange Risk

Risk neutralisation involves structuring the currency mix of the firm's assets and liabilities so that changes in exchange rates will have minimal impacts on its income, net worth, and market value.[1] The firm with a long position in the pengo can reduce its exposure by acquiring additional pengo liabilities; the firm might borrow pengos and use the loan proceeds to buy dollars or it might sell the pengo forward.[2] As a first step, the firm should estimate the impact of anticipated changes in exchange rates on its income and market value with the current mix of assets and liabilities denominated in various currencies, and then with alternative mixes of assets and liabilities denominated in these currencies.[3] This chapter describes the techniques that can be used to alter the firm's exposure to exchange risk and the costs or returns associated with such changes.[4]

LEADING AND LAGGING

Leading and lagging involves altering the currency mix of the firm's assets and liabilities by speeding or delaying payments in a foreign currency. Assume a U.S. firm holds a pengo-denominated receivable which matures in six months; at that time the firm expects to use the pengo funds obtained on repayment of the receivable to buy dollars.[5] If the pengo depreciates before the receivable matures, the firm will incur an exchange loss, $\Delta\$Y$, which is equal to the product of its long position, E_L, in the pengo, and the difference between the spot exchange rate, S_t, on the date when the receivable was acquired and the anticipated spot exchange rate on the balance-sheet date after the devaluation, S_{t+n}, or

$$\Delta\$Y = (S_t - S^*_{t+n})E_L$$

Because the exchange rate on $t+n$ is uncertain, the exchange loss can only be estimated at time t.[6]

To avoid the possible loss, the firm can reduce the value of its pengo-denominated assets to the value of its pengo-denominated liabilities, or it can increase its pengo liabilities. No exchange loss or gain would then result from a change in the exchange rate, for the firm would then have a 'square' position in the pengo; if the pengo then depreciates, the decline in the dollar value of its pengo receivable is matched by the decline in the dollar value of the pengo liabilities. Thus the firm acquires an exposed short position, E_S, to offset its exposed long position, so that

$$(S_t - S^*_{t+n})E_S = (S_t - S^*_{t+n})E_L$$

This technique is known as 'leading and lagging' or 'borrowing-and-lending'; the term 'operating hedge' is sometimes used. One variant is that the firm matches its pengo assets with liabilities denominated in a currency whose foreign exchange value is expected to remain more or less unchanged relative to the pengo, even as the pengo appreciates or depreciates relative to the dollar. Another is that the maturity of liabilities sold to hedge the exposure may be shorter than that of the receivable, so that the firm may be obliged to renew its foreign currency loans when they mature.

FORWARD EXCHANGE CONTRACTS

A second technique to alter the exposure of the firm involves transactions in forward contracts. To hedge its long position, the firm sells the pengo forward, matching the amount and maturity date of the forward contracts with the amount and maturity date of the receivable. If the pengo depreciates before the receivable matures, the decrease in the dollar value of the pengo receivable approximates the decrease in the dollar value of the pengo liability in the forward contract:[7]

$$(S_t - S^*_{t+n})E_L^S = (F_t - S^*_{t+n})E_S^F$$

The superscripts indicate whether the long and short positions involve spot or forward commitments. If F_t and S_t differ, the amount of the short forward position, as measured in pengos, required to hedge fully the receivable differs from the face value of the receivable.

Forward contracts are not generally available for maturities of more than one or two years, and even then in only a few currencies. Hence an exposure based on a long-term receivable can be hedged only by leading and lagging. In many countries, however, long-term loans may not be available, so the firm may have to combine a series of short-term loans or a series of short-term forward contracts. As each loan or forward contract matures, the firm acquires a replacement. The risk is that the interest rates on the loans may increase as they are renewed; similarly, the discount or premium on the new forward contracts may increase.

COMMODITY HEDGES

The third approach to altering exposure involves the acquisition of commodities or non-financial assets whose pengo prices are expected to change as the foreign exchange value of the pengo changes. The Ruthenian subsidiary might borrow pengos and use the loan proceeds to buy lead, tin, land or other non-financial assets in Ruthenia whose pengo prices are expected to increase as the pengo depreciates.

The more nearly the pengo prices of these non-financial assets increase in proportion to the change in the foreign exchange value of the pengo, the larger the revaluation gain from ownership of the commodity. Thus, the revaluation gain is

$$\Delta R_p = (P_{t+n} - P_t)C$$

where ΔR_p refers to the revaluation gain of the subsidiary in pengos, P_{t+n} the price of the commodity after the change in the exchange rate, P_t the spot price, and C the size of the position in this commodity. To minimise its loss from a change in the exchange rate, the firm would set ΔR_p^*, the anticipated revaluation gain, equal to the anticipated percentage change in the pengo price of the dollar. Such hedges are useful only if the capital gain from the increase in the price of the commodity exceeds the financing costs, or the opportunity costs, of the funds committed to the transaction.

The value of commodity hedges which the firm must acquire to alter its exposure by a given amount depends on the relation between the anticipated change in the local currency prices of the non-financial assets, the change in the exchange rate, and the interest rate on local currency loans; the smaller the increase in the local currency price of these assets relative to the change in the exchange rate, the larger the volume of commodity hedges the firm must acquire to effect any desired change in the income of its subsidiary. The more responsive interest rates are to anticipated changes in exchange rates, the larger the volume of commodity hedges necessary to effect the same change in the firm's exposure, since the financing costs of the commodity hedge will be higher. If both Purchasing Power Parity and Fisher Open are valid in the short run, the cost of the commodity hedge would equal the gain, and the technique provides no scope for changing the firm's exposure.

Commodity hedges are more cumbersome than leading and lagging and forward contracts. Transactions costs of commodity hedges also are higher. In addition, storage costs may be incurred. Commodity prices are uncertain, and the prices of non-financial assets are not likely to increase in proportion to changes in exchange rates, especially in the short run. Hence commodity hedges are likely to be used only if forward contracts are unavailable and leading and lagging is constrained by exchange controls or other regulations.

Acquisition of commodity futures contracts is an alternative to acquisition of the commodity. Futures contracts are commitments to deliver or receive standardised amounts of given products, such as wheat, tin and silver, at specified future dates. For example, a long position in sterling might be hedged by taking on a long position in tin, or zinc, or silver futures in London – indeed in any commodity whose sterling price is expected to rise if sterling depreciates.[8] The transactions costs associated with commodity futures are lower than those with commodities; moreover, storage costs are avoided.

THE COSTS OF ALTERING EXCHANGE EXPOSURE

Altering the exposure of any firm involves a reshuffling of assets and liabilities denominated in various currencies. In deciding on its exposure, the firm must determine whether the prices at which it can trade assets are high or low relative to the anticipated changes in exchange rates.

To estimate the change in its income from altering its exposure, the firm must anticipate the exchange rate at the end of the relevant investment period. The change in income associated with a change in the firm's exposure is the sum of the change in the exchange gain or loss plus the change in either the cumulative interest agio or the gain or loss on its forward contracts; this change in income may be positive or negative. Hence a change in exposure may not incur a cost in the traditional sense but, instead, may have a positive return – which is why some investors speculate from time to time. Initially the change in income can only be anticipated; the actual change will depend on how closely the firm's anticipations are realised.[9]

Assume the firm alters its exposure by forward exchange transactions effected at the forward rate, F_t. The anticipated cost of altering its exposure is the difference between F_t and S^*_{t+n}, where S^*_{t+n} is the anticipated spot exchange rate at the end of the investment period. If $F_t = S^*_{t+n}$ – if the firm believes that Fisher Open will hold – no anticipated cost is attached to its changing exposure. Altering the firm's exposure affects its income only if the forward rate differs from the anticipated spot rate. If $F_t \neq S^*_{t+n}$ – if the firm anticipates that deviations from Fisher Open are likely in the near future – changes in the currency mix of its assets and liabilities will alter its income.[10] If its anticipations are realised, its income will be unaltered only if $F_t = S_{t+n}$. The firm may sell the pengo forward even though the forward rate is below the anticipated spot rate, despite the anticipated cost, on the rationale that it wishes to avoid the uncertainty about the future spot rate – and the larger loss should the pengo depreciate more rapidly than it expects.[11]

If the firm alters its exposure by changing the currency denomination of its money holdings, the change in its income is the difference between the spot exchange rate, S_t, on the date at which the initial foreign exchange transaction occurs, and the anticipated spot exchange rate at the close of the investment period, S^*_{t+n}.[12] The anticipated cost of altering its exposure is, in percentage terms, $(S_t - S^*_{t+n})/S_t$.

If the firm alters its exposure by shifting the currency mix of its interest-earning assets, the anticipated change in its income is the difference between the change in its net interest income and the anticipated change in the spot exchange rate during the investment period, $(r_f - r_d) - (S_t - S^*_{t+n})$, or, in percentage terms,

$$(r_f - r_d) - \left(\frac{S_t - S^*_{t+n}}{S_t}\right)$$

A similar statement can be made if the firm alters the currency mix of its liabilities.[13]

The anticipated change in income from using commodity hedges is the difference between the anticipated change in the spot exchange rate during the interval when the firm holds the commodity and the anticipated profit on the commodity hedge. Thus

$$\left(\frac{p^*-c}{c}\right)-\left(\frac{S_t-S^*_{t+n}}{S_t}\right)$$

where $(p^*-c)/c$ represents the anticipated percentage change in the value of the commodity during the relevant investment period.

If both financial markets and commodity markets are competitive, it might be inferred that there are no bargains in the markets for assets; all assets would be appropriately priced and one form of hedging would be as good as another. Indeed, changing the currency mix of the firm's assets and liabilities would not alter its anticipated income because the anticipated changes in exchange rates would already have been 'priced away' and fully reflected in the interest agios and the exchange agios.

Thus changing the currency mix of the firm's assets and liabilities would affect the components of its income, but not its total income; so that, by reducing its long position in a weak currency, its interest income will be smaller and its exchange losses will also be smaller. However, frequently the prices of certain financial assets are controlled or regulated. Pegging the exchange rate may mean that central banks sell foreign exchange at artificially low prices if their currencies are overvalued; the firms able to buy foreign exchange at these rates get bargains. Several central banks have occasionally supported their currencies in the forward market to reduce the forward discounts; in effect these central banks subsidise the changes in the currency mix of firms' assets and liabilities.

In many countries the financial structure is managed so that lenders implicitly subsidise borrowers. Interest rates charged to borrowers may be lower than those warranted by the rate of increase in the commodity price levels, especially in the early stages of inflation. Lenders are taxed, either deliberately or because the authorities delay the adjustments of both their regulatory practices and the interest rate ceilings to increases in the commodity price level. Borrowers may wish to sell more loans to the banks at these low interest rates than the banks can buy; a queue may develop among the borrowers, and some credit demands may go unsatisfied.

If both exchange rates and interest rates are regulated, the firm can choose which of the implicit subsidies is larger. When the central bank pegs the forward exchange rate, forward exchange contracts may be cheaper than leading and lagging, unless the domestic interest rates to borrowers also are subsidised. Alternatively, when interest rates to borrowers are subsidised and the forward exchange rate is a free price, then leading and lagging may be less costly. The relative costs of these alternative approaches to altering exposure are likely to change as a devaluation appears more likely; the costs of forward contracts are likely to increase relative to the costs of leading and lagging.

The costs to an individual firm of changing its exposure may be an increasing function of the magnitude of the intended change. The net interest cost the firm pays when it leads and lags may increase as its bank loans increase. Its ability to buy forward contracts at the prevailing price also is not infinite.

ALTERING EXPOSURE TO POLITICAL RISK

The firm is concerned that the exchange controls currently applied by some countries may prevent the repatriation of funds from its foreign subsidiaries to home office; it is also concerned that some countries might tighten their controls in the future or even expropriate its subsidiaries. Leading and lagging automatically alters the firm's exposure to political risk as well as its exposure to exchange risk. The firm can hedge political risk by borrowing more within Ruthenia and then selling the pengo funds to buy dollar deposits from banks outside Ruthenia. The firm reduces its exposure to loss from changes in various regulations; if the subsidiary is expropriated, or if exchange controls are introduced, the parent may refuse to repay the loan until the host-country government provides appropriate compensation.

Forward contracts may enable firms to specialise in carrying either political risk or exchange risk. For example, a U.S. firm which wishes to alter its long position in the pengo can lead-and-lag, or it can sell the pengo forward. If the firm borrows pengos and uses the loan proceeds to buy dollar assets, it may be able to alter its exposure to both exchange risk and political risk at the same time if the dollar assets are shifted from Ruthenia. If instead the firm sells the pengo forward, it hedges the exchange risk but not the political risk. If the host-country government tightens controls on the outflow of capital, the subsidiary may not be able to remit its funds abroad. If the firm wants to avoid political risk but not the exchange risk, it might lead and lag and shift funds from Ruthenia and, at the same time, buy the pengo forward. The spot sale and the forward purchase of the pengo have offsetting impacts on its exposure to exchange risk, while its exposure to political risk has been changed by shifting assets outside Ruthenia's jurisdiction.

In many cases shifts of funds across borders are constrained by existing controls. Assume the firm has generated funds in Ruthenia from profits and depreciation which are large relative to its financial needs in Ruthenia; it would prefer to remit these funds to its home office or to some other subsidiary but is prevented from doing so by exchange controls. The interest rates on money-market investments in Ruthenia are regulated and held at a low level. The firm may be able to lend its pengos to a non-resident firm contemplating an investment in Ruthenia in exchange for a loan in dollars or some other currency outside Ruthenia; the interest rate on the pengo loan probably exceeds that on the dollar loan, but remains below the pengo interest rate consistent with the rate of inflation in Ruthenia. In some cases controls might limit or prevent these 'back-to-back' credits.

SUMMARY

A variety of techniques can be used to neutralise and hedge exchange risk and political risk, either separately or together. Leading and lagging hedges exposure to both the exchange risk and the political risk if domestic banks are used; if external currency banks are used, then these risks may be neutralised separately. Forward contracts alter exposure to exchange risk, as may commodity hedges. Each technique for altering exposure affects the firm's anticipated income.

The calculation of changes in income associated with altering exposure involves estimation of the spot exchange rate at the end of the investment period; an important element in the change in income is the anticipated change in the exchange rate. Competitive forces might be expected to equalise the costs of alternative ways of altering exposure. Various government measures may subsidise some techniques.

9. Exchange Exposure in a Multiple Currency World

The measurement of the firm's exposure to exchange risk involves estimating how various benchmarks of its economic performance – income, net worth and market value – would be affected by changes in exchange rates. Many firms indicate that they prefer not to be exposed. But there is less than complete agreement on the currency mix of assets and liabilities that is consistent with a non-exposed position.

Usually the firm estimates its exposure using information prepared in conformity with the recommendations of various accounting groups.[1] At periodic intervals the accountants prepare balance sheets and income statements for the shareholders, bankers and tax authorities.[2] If the firm has foreign subsidiaries, their assets and liabilities must be consolidated with those of the parent; consolidation recognises that the firm is a single economic entity rather than a group of separate, albeit associated, legal entities. Consolidation requires that the accountants translate the values of the assets and liabilities denominated in foreign currencies into U.S. dollars.[3]

The usual approach towards measurement of exposure is based on the accounting approach towards consolidation. In preparing balance sheets and income statements, the accountants use straightforward techniques for consistent reporting, so that the scope for arbitrary actions and for ambiguous interpretation is minimal. The central element in the accounting approach to exposure measurement involves choosing the exchange rates to use in translating the values of assets and liabilities denominated in foreign currencies into dollars.

In contrast, economists estimate exposure directly on the basis of information about the systematic relationships among changes in exchange rates, interest rates on similar assets denominated in different currencies, and changes in commodity price levels in different countries.[4] The economists want to determine how changes in exchange rates at future dates are likely to affect the income and market value of the firm. They have more of a future orientation than the accountants; the

102

economists compare the income and market value of a firm which holds assets and liabilities denominated in foreign currencies when exchange rates change with its income and market value if it holds the same currency mix of assets and liabilities and exchange rates do not change.

This chapter first considers the estimation of the firm's exposure in terms of balance-sheet analysis; the approach is the same for a firm with numerous foreign subsidiaries and for a trading firm with assets and liabilities denominated in one or two foreign currencies. The various accounting approaches to estimation of exposure are compared, and then the economic approach to exposure is discussed, together with the relation between accounting exposure and economic exposure. Finally, the recent recommendations of the Financial Accounting Standards Board for the measurement of exposure are appraised.

ACCOUNTING APPROACHES TO EXPOSURE

The primary determinant of the measurement of exposure by accountants is the choice of the exchange rate to use when translating assets and liabilities, and revenues and expenses, denominated in various foreign currencies into domestic currency. Over the last decade the accounting approach towards the selection of the exchange rate for translation of various balance-sheet items has been in flux. In the mid-1970s the most accepted position was:

> Calculating the exposure at any given date is mainly a matter of segregating the assets and liabilities on the balance sheet in such a way as to bring to light the net amount of assets that are subject to a decrease in value in the event of currency deterioration. Cash and local currency receivables are the most exposed assets. Property and plant accounts are usually considered as not exposed, on the generally accepted assumption that their value will usually rise in proportion to the devaluation of the local currency. The same theory applies to inventories to some degree, depending on whether the inventories are subject to price controls. Inventories not subject to price controls can generally be treated for this purpose in the same way as are property and plant, that is, excluded from the calculation. On the other hand, inventories subject to price control might conservatively be handled in the same way as cash for an internal management report.[5]

The first step in calculating the firm's exposure involves choosing the exchange rate to use in translating each of the entries in the balance-sheet and income statements of the foreign subsidiary into the currency of the parent. Both the historic exchange rate, that which prevailed on the date when the item entered the balance sheet, and the current rate, that on the date when the balance sheet is constructed, have been used for different balance-sheet items.[6] The firm's exposure is the sum of the values for the balance-sheet items translated at the current exchange rate. If the value of the assets translated at the current exchange rate exceeds the value of the liabilities translated at this rate, the firm has a long position in the local currency (and, by definition, a short position in the dollar). Table 9.1 shows the impacts of exchange rate changes on the firm's net worth under alternative assumptions about the values of the assets and liabilities translated at the current exchange rate.

TABLE 9.1 Impact of Exchange Rate Changes on Net Worth of Parent

Change in the price of dollar in terms of foreign currency	Summed foreign currency values translated at current exchange rate		
	Assets > Liabilities	Assets = Liabilities	Assets < Liabilities
Increase	Decrease	No impact	Increase
Decrease	Increase	No impact	Decrease

The recommendations of various accounting bodies for translation of major balance-sheet items are shown in Table 9.2. An H is placed in the cell for the balance-sheet item if the authority recommends that the historic exchange rate be used for translation, a C if the current exchange rate should be used.[7]

Until 1965 the American Institute for Certified Public Accountants (AICPA) recommended that current assets and liabilities be translated at the current exchange rate and that non-current assets and liabilities be translated at the historic exchange rate; this set of recommendations is headed AICPA I.[8] Subsequently the AICPA recommended that long-term monetary assets and liabilities be translated at the current exchange rate; under AICPA II, all monetary assets and liabilities were to be translated at the current exchange rate, and plant and equipment was to be translated at the historic rate.[9-11] The major changes were that both long-term receivables and liabilities were to be translated at the current rate, whereas before the historic rate was used for these non-current items.

TABLE 9.2 Translation Exchange Rates for Balance-Sheet Entries

	AICPA I	*AICPA II*	*FASB*
Assets			
Cash	C	C	C
Current receivables	C	C	C
Long-term receivables	H	C	C
Inventories	C	C	H
Plant and equipment	H	H	H
Liabilities			
Current liabilities	C	C	C
Long-term liabilities	H	C	C
Capital: paid in	H	H	H
retained	H	H	H

Under both approaches, the capital account entries in the subsidiary's balance sheet, both paid-in capital and retained earnings, were to be translated at the historic exchange rate. Changes in the net worth of the subsidiary in the local currency were reflected in a change in the entry for retained earnings and, consequently, a change in the value of the capital account item in the balance sheet of the parent.[12]

Finally, the current exchange rate was to be used when translating the revenues and expenses of the foreign subsidiary, as well as its profits and losses, into domestic currency.[13] The translation of revenues and expenses might occur monthly. The use of the current rate for translation should be distinguished from the amount of foreign income to be translated, which is likely to vary as the exchange rate changes.[14]

In 1975 the Financial Accounting Standards Board (FASB) proposed that all U.S. firms follow the same approach in translation.[15] The FASB made two substantive recommendations. One was that monetary assets and liabilities should be translated at the current exchange rate while non-monetary assets, both inventories and plant and equipment, should be translated at the exchange rates in effect on 'the dates to which the money prices refer', usually the historic rates.[16] The second is that exchange gains and losses should be recognised in the accounting quarter in which the change in the exchange rate occurs; before, the usual practice was that exchange losses were recognised when they were incurred, while exchange gains were recognised only when realised — when the financial asset matured or the financial liability was paid.[17,18]

It has been asserted that the FASB recommendations increase the

106 *Exchange Risk and Corporate International Finance*

divergence between accounting exposure and economic exposure, and that a firm might have a long economic exposure in a foreign currency and, at the same time, a short accounting exposure.[19,20] It is also argued that following the FASB recommendations increases the variations in the firm's reported income, given the pattern of changes in exchange rates under floating rate regimes, and that the costs of adjusting the currency mix of assets and liabilities to reduce these variations are significant. These questions are considered at the end of the next section. Neither logical analysis nor armchair reasoning is especially convincing in resolving whether the FASB recommendations are a significant improvement in the estimation of exposure.

THE ECONOMIC ESTIMATION OF EXPOSURE

The economic analysis of the firm's exposure is based on Purchasing Power Parity and Fisher Open; or, more precisely, on deviations from these propositions. If Purchasing Power Parity is continuously valid, then the non-monetary assets of the firm are not effectively exposed, since changes in the local currency price of the dollar and changes in the local currency value of the firm's holdings of plant and equipment, inventories and other non-monetary assets, are equal in amount and offsetting. Similarly, if Fisher Open is continuously valid, the exchange loss on monetary assets denominated in a currency which is depreciating that results from using the current exchange rate for translation should approximate the cumulative interest agio from the excess of foreign interest rates over U.S. interest rates; again, the firm is not effectively exposed. While the firm is exposed in the literal sense because assets and liabilities do not match by currency, it is not exposed in the economic sense, for its income and net worth will not be affected by changes in exchange rates. Similarly, its anticipated income will not be affected by changes in the exchange rate, for the income in foreign currencies will increase at the same rate as these currencies depreciate.

Estimating the firm's economic exposure involves two steps. The first step, valuation, involves anticipating the values in the host country's currency of the various items in the subsidiary's balance sheet, including monetary assets and liabilities, such as cash, receivables and accounts payable, and non-monetary assets, primarily plant and equipment and inventory, following a change in the exchange rate. Similarly, the income in the host country's currency must be anticipated for each possible value of the exchange rate.

The second step, translation, involves deciding on the exchange rates to use when expressing in U.S. dollars the values of assets, liabilities and anticipated income denominated in the foreign currency. The historic rate or the current rate might be used for translation, as well as an average of these values.

The impacts on the firm's net worth of several combinations of valuation and translation choices when the local currency depreciates are shown in Tables 9.3, 9.4 and 9.5. Table 9.3 indicates the impact on the net worth of a firm with a Ruthenian subsidiary which owns non-monetary assets when Purchasing Power Parity is valid continuously, so that changes in the pengo value of these assets are proportional to changes in the pengo price of the dollar. Valuation might be on the basis of either historic cost or current market value; the historic exchange rate or the current exchange rate might be used for translation. The Purchasing Power Parity assumption means that the combination of current valuation and the current exchange rate leads to the same anticipated impact on the parent's net worth as the combination of historic valuation and the historic exchange rate.

TABLE 9.3 Anticipated Impact on Net Worth of Currency Depreciation: Non-Monetary Assets

Translation exchange rate	Valuation of assets	
	Historic	*Current*
Historic	No change	Increase
Current	Decreases	No change

If Purchasing Power Parity does not hold, and historic values are used for both valuation and translation, the firm's net worth remains unchanged, even as the pengo depreciates. In contrast, if current values are used for both valuation and translation, then the firm's net worth decreases if the depreciation of the pengo is larger, in percentage terms, than the increase in the value of the asset in terms of the pengo. The change in the firm's net worth is the product of the difference between these two percentage rates and the historic value of the asset in terms of the pengo.

Table 9.4 shows the impact on the parent's net worth if it holds a pengo-denominated monetary asset and the pengo depreciates, on the assumption that the change in the exchange rate has been fully reflected

TABLE 9.4 Anticipated Impact on Net Worth of Currency Depreciation: Monetary Assets Unadjusted

Translation exchange rate	Valuation of assets	
	Historic	Current
Historic	No change	No change
Current	Decreases	Decreases

in the interest agio; since Fisher Open holds, the pengo value of the monetary asset is not affected by the change in the exchange rate. The net worth of the firm remains unchanged if the firm translates the pengo values at the historic exchange rate. If, however, the current exchange rate is used for translation, the firm's net worth declines. The responses in the cells in Table 9.4 differ from those in the comparable cells in Table 9.3 because the current values and historic values differ in the former table, whereas they are identical in the latter.

TABLE 9.5 Anticipated Impact on Net Worth of Currency Depreciation: Monetary Assets Adjusted

Translation exchange rate	Valuation of assets	
	Historic	Current
Historic	No change	Increase
Current	Decreases	No change

Table 9.5 shows the impact on the parent's net worth if it holds a pengo-denominated asset whose value increases through the continuous compounding of interest. If Fisher Open holds, the rate of depreciation of the pengo and the rate of increase in the pengo value of the financial asset are the same, so the responses in the cells in Table 9.5 are identical with those in the comparable cells in Table 9.3.

For the economist, the firm's anticipated income and market value will be affected by changes in exchange rates only if there are anticipated deviations from Purchasing Power Parity and Fisher Open. Since the relations between the changes in exchange rates and both changes in the local currency price of non-monetary assets and the interest rates on similar assets denominated in different currencies are uncertain, exposure can only be estimated. One approach – an extreme one – is to assert that because the proportionality propositions appear empirically valid, the firm is not exposed. But this view, even if supported by data for the past, may not be convincing for the future.[21] Moreover, even if the proportionality propositions are accepted as valid long-run tendencies, deviations from these propositions are certain in the short run. The size of these deviations – and their duration – must be estimated.

Some firms – those which produce exports or import-competing goods, or have income in foreign currencies from licensing, royalty and rental agreements – may have an income exposure even though they do not hold significant amounts of assets and liabilities denominated in foreign currencies.[22] Estimation of exposure in terms of deviations from the proportionality propositions integrates exposure of the items in the income statement with the exposure of balance-sheet items. Thus, changes in the firm's net interest income as it alters the currency mix of its assets and liabilities can be integrated with, and perhaps offset against, exchange losses on assets and liabilities denominated in foreign currencies.

The economic approach to estimating the firm's exposure involves separate estimates for non-monetary assets, for monetary assets and liabilities, and for anticipated income streams – the profit projections of the foreign subsidiaries. The anticipated exposure on non-monetary assets is the difference between the anticipated change in the local currency value of these assets and the anticipated change in the exchange rate. Formally,

$$E^*_{nm} = (\Delta P^* - \Delta E^*)A$$

where E^*_{nm} is the anticipated percentage change in the local currency price of the asset, ΔP^* the anticipated percentage change in the local currency price of the asset, ΔE^* the anticipated percentage change in the exchange rate over the same time-interval, and A the local currency value of the asset at historic cost. The procedure requires estimates of both the anticipated change in the local currency price of non-monetary assets and the anticipated change in the exchange rate.

The firm may estimate its exposure for the next quarter, the next year, or the next quinquennium; the size of the exposed position appears likely to vary with the interval of observation. That Purchasing Power Parity has greater validity in the long run means that the difference in the values for the anticipated percentage change in the local currency value of the asset and the anticipated percentage change in the exchange rate are usually smaller over long intervals than over shorter intervals.

The anticipated exposure on monetary assets and liabilities denominated in a foreign currency is the difference between the anticipated exchange loss or gain from translating the net position in this currency into domestic currency at the anticipated spot exchange rate and the cumulative interest agio during the same investment period.[23] Thus,

$$E_m = (r_f - r_d)B - \Delta \dot{E}^*\, B$$

where E_m is the dollar value of exposure on monetary assets, $(r_f - r_d)$ the interest agio, B the net position in foreign currency, and $\Delta \dot{E}^*$ the anticipated percentage change in the exchange rate.[24] The size of the exposed position varies with the interval for which exposure is estimated; in general, the longer the interval, the more likely that the cumulative interest agio will offset the anticipated exchange loss.

Similarly, the firm's anticipated exposure on its expected income in foreign currencies is measured by the dollar equivalent of the difference between the percentage change in the local currency revenues and costs as the exchange rate changes. The local currency profits of foreign subsidiaries would be expected to increase when the currencies of the countries in which these subsidiaries are located depreciate, so the dollar value of these profits are likely to remain unaffected in the long run if not in the short run. Deviations from this extension of the proportionality propositions may occur because the local currency selling price for final output may increase less rapidly than the local currency price of the dollar, at least for a year or two, perhaps because price ceilings limit the rate at which selling prices can be increased. No general statement can be made about the time-dimension of the relationship between changes in the exchange rates and changes in selling prices, revenues and expenses. The firm may have a substantial economic exposure on its income statement even after it has matched the currency mix of assets and liabilities, and so minimising the changes in income attributable to changes in the exchange rate may require that assets and liabilities denominated in the foreign currency differ in value.

The economic exposure of the firm is the sum of its exposures on non-monetary assets, monetary assets and liabilities, and anticipated income streams. Although the force of the proportionality propositions is that the firm is not exposed in economic terms in the long run because the interest rate differentials reflect changes in exchange rates, the firm may choose to arrange the currency mix of its monetary assets so that its economic exposure in the short run is minimal.[25]

RECONCILING THE ACCOUNTING AND THE ECONOMIC ESTIMATES OF EXPOSURE

The thrust of the economic approach is that the firm is not exposed in the long run, regardless of the currency mix of its assets and liabilities, but that it is unlikely that it would not be exposed in the short run. The thrust of the accounting approach is that the firm is exposed only if the sum of assets to be translated at the current exchange rate differs from the sum of liabilities to be translated at the current rate. One shortcoming of the accounting approach is that the choice of exchange rates for translation is arbitrary; another, that the impact of changes in exchange rate on the domestic value of foreign income streams is neglected.

Even though the firm is non-exposed by the currently accepted set of accounting recommendations for the exchange rates for translation, the firm will be exposed in economic terms in the short run. In the long run, the firm could be non-exposed in accounting terms as well as in economic terms. If the firm should arrange the currency mix of its assets and liabilities so as to minimise its economic exposure in the short run, then it will almost certainly increase its accounting exposure. This dilemma is unavoidable. The managers must decide whether they prefer to minimise the variations in reported income, at the cost of larger variations in actual income, or to minimise the variations in actual income, at the cost of larger variations in reported income.

THE IMPACT OF FASB RECOMMENDATIONS

The managers of many U.S. firms initially were critical of the FASB exposure recommendations. While the idea that all U.S. firms would follow a similar approach in reporting exchange gains and losses was accepted, the recommendation that all exchange gains and losses be reported quarterly, regardless of whether they were realised, was criticised, for it ruled out the use of an internal reserve to dampen the impact of exchange losses and gains on reported profits on a yearly and especially on a quarterly basis. The recommendations about the exchange rates to use in translation of particular balance-sheet items into dollars, especially that inventories be translated at the historic rate rather than at the current rate, was also criticised.[26] The adoption of the second recommendation alone meant that the dollar equivalent of earnings of foreign subsidiaries would tend to vary with any cyclical pattern in exchange rate movements, given the existing currency mix of the firm's assets and liabilities. The logical implication of both recommendations is that the firm should make a one-time adjustment of its assets and liabilities if it wishes to reduce the cyclical variations in its reported income caused by changes in exchange rates.

If the firm had arranged the currency mix of assets and liabilities so that it had a non-exposed position prior to the FASB recommendations when inventories were translated at the current exchange rate, it will have a short position in the foreign currency post-FASB because of the requirement that inventories be translated at the historic exchange rate. The firm can achieve the same accounting exposure in the post-FASB period as it had prior to FASB by reducing its debt denominated in the foreign currency by the amount of subsidiary's inventories; in general, a one-time adjustment is required.[27]

Since interest rates on loans denominated in most foreign currencies are higher than interest rates on comparable dollar loans, the reduction in debt denominated in foreign currencies should reduce the firm's net interest payments.[28] Hence anticipated income of the firm might be expected to increase slightly as a result of the reduction of total debt denominated in foreign currencies; moreover, the variations in reported income would be smaller.[29]

The firm might choose to be non-exposed by the currently accepted accounting recommendations because predictions of changes in exchange rates appear to lead to random rather than systematic profits — in the short run, forward exchange rates and the interest rate differentials are unbiased predictors of future changes in exchange rates. Unless the firm has some way of predicting future spot exchange rates more accurately than the other investors as a group, e.g. unless its forecasts are superior to the forecasts implicit in the forward rates, consistent profits cannot be made from these predictions. Hence there is no reason why the firm should continue to maintain an exposed position according to the prevailing accounting approach.[30] Indeed, the only reason the firm's interests would be served by maintaining a currency mix of assets and liabilities considered exposed by prevailing accounting recommendations is that managers have useful information about future spot rates that the market does not have or is not using efficiently.

SUMMARY

This chapter has distinguished the economic approach to the measurement of exposure from the recommendations of various accounting groups. The thrust of the economic approach is that the exposure should be analysed in terms of deviations from Purchasing Power Parity and Fisher Open; the economists compare the firm's income if it holds assets and liabilities denominated in various foreign currencies and the exchange rate changes with its income if it holds the same currency mix of assets and liabilities and the exchange rate does not change.[31] Since, in the long run, commodity price levels and interest rate tend to move as suggested by Purchasing Power Parity and the Fisher effect, the firm's income in the long run, and presumably its market value, will not be especially sensitive to its accounting exposure, however measured. The operational consequence is that the firm can readily alter the currency mix of its assets and liabilities to minimise its exposure according to the currently preferred accounting recommendations with minimal concern that it is altering its long-run economic exposure.

10. Tax Implications of Exchange Losses and Gains

The structure of corporate income taxes may affect the willingness of the firm to maintain an exposed position in various foreign currencies and bear the uncertainty of variations in income from changes in exchange rates. Moreover, the tax structure also affects the techniques used to alter exposure, and the countries in which firms realise their exchange gains and their exchange losses.

Several aspects of U.S. taxation are relevant for the firm's attitude towards exposure. A decline in income resulting from changes in exchange rates or from measures undertaken to alter exposure reduces taxable income. Increases in income attributable to changes in exchange rates are generally taxed at the rates that apply to ordinary income; thus the profits on forward contracts are taxed at the rates that apply to ordinary income, even if the maturity of the forward contracts exceeds six months, rather than at the lower tax rate applicable to long-term capital gains.[1] Finally, exchange losses and gains affect the firm's taxable income only when the gains and losses are realised.[2]

Corporate income is fully taxed in the country where earned. Thus the Ruthenian subsidiary of a U.S. firm pays Ruthenian taxes on its Ruthenian income. The U.S. authorities tax the income of the foreign branches of U.S. firms when earned; the income of the foreign subsidiaries of U.S. firms is taxed when repatriated as dividends to the U.S. parent.[3] The U.S. parent receives a credit against its U.S. tax liability for its corporate income tax payments to the fiscal authorities abroad. The effective tax rate on foreign income may be below the rate on U.S. income if three conditions are satisfied: if the foreign tax rate is below the U.S. tax rate, the foreign activity is organised as a subsidiary rather than as a branch, and foreign income is not repatriated in the year when earned.[4] Consequently, a U.S. firm may delay repatriation of income from subsidiaries based in countries where the tax rates are

114

below the U.S. rates to delay the payment of its tax to the U.S. authorities; in effect the firm receives an interest-free loan from the U.S. tax authorities equal to its residual U.S. tax liability.

The impact of the tax structure on the exchange exposure of the firm depends on the tax rates both on ordinary income and on exchange losses and gains, and on the firm's attitudes towards variations in income resulting from exchange rate changes. The higher the tax rates on ordinary income, the smaller the change in after-tax income associated with exchange gains or losses of given amount, and the less likely that the firm will be concerned with its exposure. Corporate tax rates in the 40–50 per cent range sharply moderate the impact of changes in before-tax income on after-tax income. Nevertheless, a risk-averse firm may be reluctant to have an exposed position, despite the dampening influence of the tax structure on exchange losses, especially if the potential losses are large.

THE TAX STRUCTURE AND THE FIRM'S EXCHANGE EXPOSURE

If certain conditions hold – the firm is risk-neutral and exchange losses and gains lead to one-to-one changes in taxable income – the tax structure should not have a major impact on the firm's exposure. Yet the tax structure may affect how a firm alters its exposure if the tax rate on exchange profits on forward contracts differs from that on ordinary income. Taxation of profits on forward contracts and ordinary income at the same rate may lead a firm to 'double-hedge' – to buy forward contracts equal to twice its exposed position.[5] One explanation why a firm might double-hedge is that it equates the after-tax gain on its forward contracts with the before-tax loss on its exposed position. But this explanation is inappropriate, since the after-tax profits on the forward contracts should be compared with the after-tax loss on its exposed position. A second explanation for double-hedging is that the reported exchange loss may not reduce taxable income; the dollar value of foreign assets declines while the dollar value of foreign income remains unchanged. In this case the after-tax exchange loss is identical with the before-tax exchange loss. If the change in the exchange rate leads to an exchange loss which does not reduce taxable income, double-hedging may not be an efficient way to avoid a decline in reported income.

Assume a U.S. firm has a Ruthenian subsidiary. If the pengo is devalued, the firm may report a loss because the dollar value of pengo assets has declined. Yet the devaluation may not lead to any change in its taxable income and its corporate income tax liability. To insulate its reported income from the decline attributable to the change in the exchange rate, the firm must buy that volume of forward contracts so that the after-tax profit on the forward contracts equals the before-tax (and after-tax) decline in its reported income; if the tax rate on the exchange profits on forward contracts is 50 per cent, the firm must double-hedge.

Double-hedging may incur unnecessary costs if the proportionality concepts are valid, for the decline in the firm's net worth is apparent rather than real.[6] Assume, for example, that the subsidiary holds real assets — plant and equipment — in Ruthenia and that the pengo price of these assets rises in proportion to the depreciation of the pengo. Then the net worth of the subsidiary in pengos rises in proportion to the depreciation on the pengo and the net worth of the parent should be unaffected.

The apparent need to double-hedge arises because the increases in the pengo value of the subsidiary's assets and its net worth are not recognised. If these increases were recognised, the parent's net worth would not change as a result of the devaluation. If the firm double-hedges as a consequence, it incurs the costs associated with a redundant transaction.

Similarly, if the firm holds financial assets denominated in the pengo and the pengo depreciates, the firm may double-hedge because of the exchange loss. If Fisher Open holds, however, the net worth of the firm will not be affected by the change in the exchange rate. The firm might be better served by altering the currency mix of its assets and liabilities to reduce or eliminate its balance-sheet accounting exposure.

Neutralising exchange losses involves matching the profits on forward contracts with the loss on the exposed position on an after-tax basis. For example, assume the firm has a long position in the pengo with dollar value of E, and the spot exchange rate is S_t. If the pengo depreciates, and the end-of-period exchange rate is S_{t+n}, the dollar value of the before-tax loss is

$$\frac{(S_{t+n} - S_t)E}{S_t}$$

and the dollar value of the after-tax loss is

$$\frac{(1-t)(S_{t+n} - S_t)E}{S_t}$$

where t is the corporate tax rate. The firm might sell forward pengo contracts in anticipation that the profits on these contracts would offset the loss on its exposed position. The profit on these contracts is the product of the size of its forward exchange commitment, C, and the difference between the exchange rate, F_t, at which it buys its forward contracts and the end-of-period spot exchange rate, S_{t+n}, and the tax rate on these profits, t', or

$$\frac{(1-t')(F_t - S_{t+n})C}{S_t}$$

If exchange profits on the forward contracts are taxed at the rate t, then the volume of forward contracts, C, required to match the loss on the exposed position might seem larger than E. If the tax rates applied to profits on the forward contracts and on corporate income are the same and F_t approximates S_{t+n}^*, the after-tax exchange profits on the forward contracts would equal the after-tax exchange loss on the exposed position when the size of the forward position equals the size of the exposed position.

If F_t and S_{t+n}^* differ, perhaps because the forward pengo is at a suostantial forward discount, the value of forward contracts the firm must sell to hedge fully its exposure will exceed the value of this position because the anticipated profit per pengo on each forward contract is smaller than the loss per pengo on the exposed position. The complete hedge is

$$E' = \frac{E(S_t - S_{t+n}^*)}{(F_t - S_{t+n}^*)}$$

If the tax rate on profits on forward contracts is lower than the tax rate on corporate income, a smaller volume of forward contracts is required to hedge fully the exposed position.[7] If, at the extreme, the exchange profits on forward contracts are untaxed, then the firm can fully protect its exposed position by selling the volume of forward contracts which approximates the value of its exposed position. If t' is the tax rate on the exchange profits on forward contracts, the volume of forward contracts required to hedge fully its exposure is

$$E' = \frac{(1-t)(S_t - S_{t+n}^*)E}{(1-t')(F_t - S_{t+n}^*)}$$

For example, if the dollar equivalent of the exposed pengo position is $50, then the firm might buy $50 forward to hedge fully its exposure if the tax rates on ordinary income and on the exchange profits on forward contracts are the same. If both tax rates are 50 per cent, the decline in the after-tax income is $25, and the after-tax profit on the forward contracts is $25. If instead the tax rate on the profit on the forward contracts is 25 per cent, the firm need only buy forward contracts of $33.33 to hedge fully its exposure.

If the firm alters its exposure by leading and lagging, changes in its income are the sum of changes in its net interest payments or receipts and its exchange losses or gains. Interest payments are a tax-deductible expense. The change in the firm's after-tax income from leading and lagging is the net of the product of one minus the corporate tax rate, $1 - t$, and the difference between the interest rate on pengo loans, r_p and the interest rate on dollar loans, r_s, and the change in its exposure, ΔE, or $(1 - t)(r_p - r_s)\Delta E$, and the difference between the after-tax exchange losses as the exposure changes. To illustrate, assume the firm alters its exposure; its income changes by the net of the change in its interest payments, $r_p - r_s$, and the realised change in the exchange rate, $(S_t - S_{t+n})/S_t$, times the change in its exposure, or

$$\left((r_p - r_s) - \frac{(S_t - S_{t+n})}{S_t} \right) \Delta E$$

If Fisher Open is valid, the change in its after-tax income as a result of the change in its net interest payments, $(1 - t)(r_p - r_s)\Delta E$, equals the change in its after-tax income from the change in the exchange rate:

$$\frac{(1 - t)(S_t - S_{t+n})\Delta E}{S_t}$$

Tax considerations may affect the choice between leading and lagging and forward contracts as a way to alter exposure. If Interest Rate Parity is valid, the firm should be indifferent on a before-tax basis to the technique used to change its exposure because their costs are the same; tax considerations alone would determine which technique is preferable. If the tax rate on the exchange gains on forward contracts is the same as the tax rate on corporate income, tax considerations would not affect the choice. If the tax rate on corporate income exceeds that on the profits on forward contracts, altering exposure through the use of forward contracts is preferable if Interest Rate Parity holds. If Interest Rate Parity is not valid, then the choice of technique is determined by whether the percentage spread between the two tax rates is larger or smaller than the percentage deviation from Interest Rate Parity.

If the change in the exchange rate reduces the firm's reported income but not its taxable income, perhaps because there has been no 'taxable event', leading and lagging is likely to be the less costly way to alter exposure, unless the profits on forward contracts are not taxed. The rationale is that the size of the hedge would be smaller than the required change in the forward position.

TAXATION AND FOREIGN SUBSIDIARIES

The firm with subsidiaries in several countries is concerned with its exposure on a global basis, currency by currency. The firm must decide whether changes in exposure should be undertaken by the parent or by one of the subsidiaries. By distributing exchange gains and exchange losses among the subsidiaries in different countries as well as between the various foreign subsidiaries and the parent, the firm may be able to reduce its tax liabilities and either increase its after-tax income or reduce the volume of forward contracts required to effect a complete hedge. The trade-offs involve whether the gain on the forward contracts is better handled as foreign source income or U.S. source income,[8] and whether the exchange losses are better handled as a charge against U.S. source income or against foreign source income. For example, assume the firm has an exposed position in the pengo which it wishes to hedge. The U.S. parent might hold the long pengo position and take the exchange loss resulting from the changes in exchange rate to realise a decline in taxable U.S. income. The forward contracts might be acquired by the Ruthenian subsidiary if income on forward contracts in Ruthenia is taxed at a lower rate than in the United States; the increase in its tax payments might be less than the reduction in the U.S. tax payment.[9] Total taxes paid by the firm in the year of the exchange loss would decline. The cost of insulating income and net worth from losses due to exchange rate changes is smaller than if the forward transaction were undertaken in the United States.

SUMMARY

Changes in exchange rates may reduce the firm's taxable income. The decline in after-tax income is equal to the product of one minus the tax rate and the exchange loss. Similarly, profits on forward contracts increase taxable income; the increase in after-tax income is the product of the exchange profit and one minus the tax rate on these gains, which is usually the tax rate on corporate income.

The tax structure may affect the firm's attitude towards whether it should maintain an exposed position. The tax structure also affects whether the U.S. parent, or one of its overseas subsidiaries, should buy the forward contracts or otherwise seek to profit from having an exposed position.

11. Strategies Towards Exchange Risk

The statements of corporate managers and financial executives suggest a variety of strategies towards exchange risk. A strategy is a systematic approach indicating when an exposure in a foreign currency should be maintained, and when it should be increased or reduced. The elements in a strategy include the anticipated costs of altering exposure by transactions effected currently and at various future dates, and the firm's attitudes towards the uncertainty about impacts of changes in exchange rates and changes in exchange controls on its income, net worth, and market value.

Sometimes it is argued that corporate managers should ignore exchange risks and seek instead to maximise the firm's expected profits.[1] Then they would alter the firm's exposure as long as the anticipated change in the exchange rate differs from the interest agio or exchange agio; generally they would maintain either a long position or a short position in the foreign currency. Each investor could then decide whether to hold equities of firms whose incomes are uncertain because they maintain exposure in foreign currencies.

A strategy towards exchange risk involves a programmed approach towards deciding on the currency mix of assets and liabilities. Each strategy has its own rationale, sometimes implicit, sometimes explicit, about the returns and the risks associated with foreign currency exposure.

One strategy is risk neutralisation; the firm holds monetary assets denominated in foreign currencies and real assets abroad only on a fully hedged basis, so that it is never exposed to loss by the prevailing accounting measures from changes in the exchange rates. The rationale is that the firm is a 'specialist in marketing or production, and not in foreign exchange'. The managers may be reluctant to note losses due to exchange rate changes in the firm's annual reports.[2] The assumption implicit in this strategy is that the economic costs of maintaining a non-exposed position are low, and that the firm is not at a significant

121

disadvantage relative to its competitors who might maintain exchange exposures.[3]

Alternatively, the firm might ignore its accounting exposure in the belief that the cost of altering its exposure is a 'fair bet'. The managers believe that forward contracts are 'efficiently priced' and that interest rates on similar assets denominated in different currencies fully reflect anticipated changes in exchange rates, so that there are no unexploited profit opportunities. Those that follow this strategy either believe that Fisher Open holds in the short run as well as in the long run, or that if Fisher Open does not hold precisely in the short run, the administrative costs that would have to be incurred in attempting to minimise losses or to secure gains from changes in exchange rates are too high to warrant the effort. The currency mix of the firm's assets and liabilities would be an unplanned result of a large number of varied transactions denominated in different currencies. The managers would not be deterred from acquiring exposed positions and subjecting the firm to exchange losses, in the belief that losses and gains would be offsetting in the long run.

A third strategy involves arranging the currency mix of assets and liabilities to maintain the largest possible short position in foreign currencies; the firm borrows as much as possible abroad to finance its overseas activities, and perhaps even some of its domestic operations. The rationale is that managers believe that the interest agio is a downward-biased estimate of the prospective changes in the exchange rates – that over time, foreign currencies depreciate more rapidly than is suggested by the excess of interest rates on foreign assets and liabilities over those on dollar assets and liabilities. Those who follow this strategy believe that exchange risk and political risk are 'under-priced' – that the deviations from Fisher Open are sufficiently large so that it is preferable to incur the costs of the higher interest payments on loans denominated in foreign currencies to be able to profit from the continuous or sporadic depreciation of these currencies, and the concomitant reduction in dollar value equivalent of these loans.

A fourth strategy involves arranging the currency mix of the firm's assets and liabilities so that it maintains the largest possible long position in foreign currencies; the firm borrows domestically to finance its overseas activities and the acquisition of financial assets denominated in foreign currencies. The rationale is that the interest agio is an upward-biased estimate of the losses that might be incurred as a result of the depreciation of foreign currencies; these currencies depreciate less rapidly (or appreciate more rapidly) than is suggested by the excess of foreign interest rates over dollar interest rates.

None of these strategies requires that the managers attempt to predict the magnitude and timing of changes in exchange rates. Once a strategy has been adopted, however, the firm maintains the same position towards exposure regardless of new information about changes in monetary policies, inflation rates, exchange rates and exchange controls. Some managers might identify one strategy as appropriate for one currency, and a second for other currencies.

More complex strategies involve changes in the currency mix of the firm's assets and liabilities in response to new information about the anticipated changes in exchange rates, interest rate differentials and the exchange agios. The questions are the same: when should the firm maintain a long or a short position in a foreign currency, and when should the firm be non-exposed. These strategies may be examined in the context of one-period models and of n-period models. In one-period models the firm has a long (or short) position in a foreign currency on the first day of the period; it anticipates that a transaction will occur on the last day of the period that will neutralise its exposure. The firm has one opportunity at the beginning of the period to decide whether to retain, hedge or reverse its exposure. In the n-period models, in contrast, the firm has numerous opportunities to alter its exposure before the last day. The firm may change its exposure for the next interval, for the next several intervals, or until a transaction occurs that will neutralise its exposure. The shorter the maturities of the foreign contracts purchased to alter its exposure, the larger the number of such transactions ultimately required if the firm wishes to remain non-exposed for any given interval, and the larger the transactions costs incurred by the firm. In these models the firm is necessarily uncertain about the cost at which it may be able to alter its exposure at various future dates. The firm may purchase forward contracts with very long maturities, either to minimise the additional transactions costs associated with a series of short-term transactions, or because it anticipates that the costs of altering its exposure in the future may increase. Consequently, the firm must be concerned with the current costs of altering its exposure for intervals of varying horizons and the anticipated costs of similar transactions at future dates. The two decisions – the date on which to alter its exposure and the interval during which the altered exposure will be maintained – are interdependent.

Thus a firm might shift between several of these strategies; it might maintain a long position in a weak currency when the likelihood that the currency will depreciate sharply is low, and acquire a short position in this currency as the likelihood increases. The rationale is that the exchange agio and the interest agio are upward-biased estimates of the anticipated depreciation when the likelihood of sharp depreciation is low, and a downward-biased estimates when the likelihood is high.

A GRAPHIC EXPOSITION OF ALTERNATIVE STRATEGIES

These several strategies implicitly combine statements about the firm's attitudes towards risk and the anticipated costs of altering its exposure, where the cost is the net of changes in the interest agio (or the exchange agio) associated with a change in its exposure and the anticipated exchange gain. In this context, risk involves variations in the firm's income about its expected value from unanticipated changes in exchange rates. Firms differ in their willingness to bear risk; as a consequence, their exposures may differ, even though their estimates of the anticipated costs of changing exposure are the same. Similarly, firms with the same attitude towards risk may have different exposures because their estimates of the costs of altering exposure differ – because their anticipations of changes in exchange rates are not identical.

The decision rules for each strategy can be shown using the diagram chosen to illustrate Fisher Open. In Fig. 11.1 the interest agio and the exchange agio are measured on the vertical axis in per cent per year; the

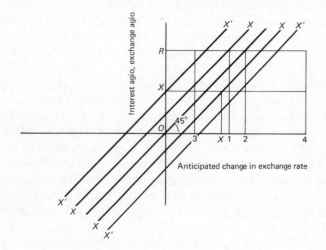

Fig. 11.1.
Graphic presentation of exchange exposure strategies.

anticipated change in the exchange rate is measured on the horizontal axis, also in terms of per cent per year. Foreign interest rates exceed domestic interest rates above the origin. The firm anticipates an increase in the price of the dollar in terms of foreign exchange to the right of the origin, e.g. the foreign currency depreciates.

The diagram illustrates whether the anticipated deviation from Fisher Open is sufficiently large to justify maintaining a short position or a long position in a foreign currency. The 45° line represents the locus of points at which the interest agio (and the exchange agio) and the anticipated change in the exchange rate are equal. While the interest agio (or the exchange agio) is known, the change in the exchange rates can only be anticipated. The cost or return from altering exposure is the difference between the interest agio (or the exchange agio) and the anticipated change in the exchange rate; this cost or return is shown by distance to the 45° line from the intersection of a horizontal intercept to the current interest agio, and of a vertical intercept to the anticipated change in the exchange rate. For all points below the 45° line in the northeast quadrant the anticipated depreciation of the foreign currency exceeds the excess of foreign interest rates over domestic interest rates. Conversely, for all points above the 45° line in the northeast quadrant the anticipated rate of the depreciation of the foreign currency is smaller than the excess of foreign interest rates over domestic interest rates. Comparable statements can be made about intersections in the southwest quadrant.

The combination of information about the anticipated change in the exchange rate and the interest agio is inadequate to determine whether the firm should maintain an exposed position; for this purpose, information is needed on the firm's attitude towards uncertainty. Each firm's attitude towards risk can be expressed as the boundary of indifference between remaining non-exposed and being exposed; this attitude can be represented by bands about the 45° line, such as *XX*, *X'X'*, and so forth. The more risk-averse the firm, the wider the band.[4] Each firm remains or becomes exposed only if the interest agio and the anticipated change in the exchange rate differ by more than enough to dominate its risk-averseness. For example, the band might be drawn so that the difference between the interest agio and the anticipated change in the exchange rate would have to exceed 1 per cent (or 2 per cent, or 5 per cent, etc.) before the firm would maintain an exposed position.

If the excess of foreign over domestic interest rates exceeds the anticipated rate of depreciation of the foreign currency by more than the minimum required to bear the uncertainty, the firm would acquire a long position in the foreign currency. In contrast, if the excess of foreign over domestic interest rate is smaller than the anticipated depreciation of the foreign currency by more than the minimum necessary to induce the firm to maintain an exposed position, the firm would develop a short position in the foreign currency.

Assume that foreign interest rates exceed domestic interest rates by OX. If the anticipated rate of depreciation of foreign currency is smaller than OY, the risk-neutral firm would develop a long position in the foreign currency; it might sell dollar debt to get the funds to buy assets denominated in the foreign currency. If instead the anticipated rate of depreciation of the foreign currency is greater than OY, the firm would develop a short position in the foreign currency. The more risk-averse the firm, the larger the difference required between OX and OY before the firm would maintain an exposed position.

The 'cookbook' strategies can be illustrated in terms of Fig. 11.1. Assume the interest agio is OR, and the same for all firms, regardless of their exchange rate anticipations. Points 1, 2, 3 and 4 indicate the anticipated rates of depreciation of the foreign exchange by managers of different firms. The firm which is highly risk-averse believes the anticipated change in the exchange rate is represented by (1) and it maintains a non-exposed position unless the anticipated pay-off for maintaining an exposed position is extremely high; the difference between the interest agio and the anticipated change in the exchange rate must lie outside a very wide band, such as $X'X'$, before the firm would maintain an exposed position. The firm which accepts the efficient market view believes that the cost of altering exposure approximates zero because the interest agio and the anticipated change in exchange rate are offsetting; the firm which believes the anticipated change in the exchange rate is represented by (2). The firm which believes that the interest agio is an upward-biased estimate of the anticipated change in the exchange rate is represented by (3); this firm develops a long position in the foreign currency if the relevant anticipated change in the price of the foreign currency is to the left of OR. In contrast, the firm which believes that the interest agio is downward-biased and anticipates an exchange rate change represented by (4) maintains a short position in the foreign currency because its anticipated depreciation of the foreign currency is large relative to the interest rate differential. Whether the last two firms acquire and maintain an exposed position depends on whether the difference between the interest agio and the anticipated change in the exchange rate is large relative to the payment they require for maintaining an exposed position.

The decision framework is Fig. 10.1 represents a one-period decision model; an alternative approach might involve comparisons between the current costs of changing exposure and the anticipated costs of changing exposure,at various future dates. Similar figures could be developed for each future date. In the one-period model the interest costs associated with altering exposure are known; in the *n*-period models this costs must be estimated for all intervals which begin at some future date. Hence the uncertainty band might be wider for more distant dates. The anticipated gain or loss from changes in the exchange rates must be estimated, both in the one-period models and the *n*-period models; greater uncertainty may be attached to the estimates for the more distant dates.

The size of the firm's exposed position is a policy variable under the control of the firm. Two factors limit the size of the firm's exposure. One, internal to the firm, is that the utility to the firm of the additional income from maintaining a long position in a currency which might appreciate or a short position in a currency which might depreciate may decline as its income rises; the gains in utility may be less than proportional to the gains in income, even if the gains in income are directly proportional to changes in exposure. A second, external to the firm, is that the cost of altering its exposed position may increase more rapidly than the change in its exposed position, perhaps because the interest rate charged the firm as it alters its exposure increases, the larger the amount of borrowing incurred by the firm. Thus, the more than proportional decline in the utility from the expected gain limits the magnitude of the change in the firm's exposure as its anticipations of the future exchange rates change.

EXPLICIT DECISION MODELS

Several decision models have been advanced by various analysts.[5] One developed in the context of the pegged exchange rate system, recommends that the decisions about exposure be a function of the probable loss from a change in the exchange rate, the probable error of the forecast (represented by one plus the forecaster's error percentage), and the corporate risk factor (represented by one plus a decimal which represents the risk-averseness of the firm).[6] For example, if the estimate of the probable loss is 20 per cent, that for the error of the forecast 10 per cent and that for the risk factor 15 per cent, the firm would hedge its exposed position whenever the interest agio is less than $(0.20 \times 1.10 \times 1.15) = 2.75$ per cent. In the absence of forecast errors, a risk-neutral firm would move to a non-exposed position whenever the interest agio is less than the probable loss; the introduction of a term for the forecast error means the firm might maintain a non-exposed position even though the probable loss is less than the interest agio. As the interest agio increases relative to the probable loss, more and more firms might find the cost of moving to a non-exposed position too high.

The unique element in this model is explicit recognition of the forecaster's success in determining the firm's policy towards exposure. The larger or the more frequent the forecaster's errors in the past, the larger the upward adjustment in the probable loss, and the more likely the firm will hedge its exposure. Since forecast errors are inevitable, at issue is whether the forecaster's error should be recognised independently from the risk-averseness of the firm, or whether the risk-averseness includes the uncertainty implicit in the forecast error. In the world of certainty there is no risk; the firm's decisions about exposure would be determined uniquely by the relationship between the interest agio and the anticipated change in the exchange rate. The firm is risk-averse because of forecast errors. Adding the forecast error to the measure of risk-averseness to determine the boundary for altering exposure moves the firms towards a non-exposed position if the forecaster has a history of errors, and so the firm may pay unnecessarily high costs to move to a non-exposed position.[7]

An alternative approach towards exposure management is based on the risk and return models used in the study of equity markets.[8] These models are concerned with the increase in the firm's income from bearing uncertainty, in the sense of the variability of the income streams around anticipated levels. To maximise its return, the firm should seek to minimise the costs of altering its exposure, which is net of the difference in the interest agio, interest rates and exchange losses or gains. The exchange loss or gain is the mean of a probability distribution of future exchange rates and hence an estimated value; the costs of neutralising or hedging the risk are known values for all periods that start today and estimated values for all subsequent periods. Both the risk of the change in the exchange rate and future hedging costs are estimated values. The firm also wants to minimise the uncertainty associated with changes in the exchange rate and the costs of altering its exposure at some future date. The less risk-averse the firm, the more nearly the model resembles a simple cost-minimisation model; if the firm is risk-neutral, the model is simply then a cost-minimisation model. Hence the usefulness of the model depends primarily on the ability of the managers to identify the upper limit to the costs they will incur to avoid uncertainty.

The test of any model is its performance – how well it predicts. The models can be ranked against the past data. However, these *ex post* comparisons encounter the problem that some strategies require the firm to be exposed at some times and not at others and there are no effective decision rules indicating when the exposed position should have been changed. So the more complex strategies cannot be readily tested.

SUMMARY

The various strategies towards exchange risk incorporate the firm's attitude towards uncertainty and the costs of altering the firm's exposure. More complex models involve several future periods; the firm may increase or reduce its exposure as its estimates of the costs of changing exposure vary. In these models the firm must anticipate future changes in the interest agio and the exchange agio.

The primary input of the firm in its policy towards exchange risk is its own attitude towards the uncertainty of variations in income levels from changes in the exchange rate. Someone within the firm must determine how it will be affected by changes in exchange rates and decide whether it should maintain a non-exposed position so as to reduce its susceptibility to losses from changes in exchange rates.

The second input to the firm's decision is the cost of altering its exposure. While the interest agio and the exchange agio are known for today's transactions, they must be estimated for future transactions; the changes in exchange rates must be anticipated. The firm needs a set of exchange rate forecasts and a capability for deciding when the probable change in the exchange rate is significantly different from the probable change that might be inferred from the interest agio or the exchange agio.

12. The Firm, Exchange Risk and Political Risk: A General Approach

The firm involved in international business encounters a unique set of risks. The timing of changes in both exchange rates and in exchange controls is unknown. Governments announce that they will not change their parities, or that they will rely on floating exchange rates for the indefinite future, or that they will not adopt or alter their exchange controls, or that the property rights of foreign firms will be respected. Such commitments may be maintained – for a time. But national monetary policies and national politics are in more or less continuous flux; governments come and go, and successor regimes may not feel bound by the commitments of their predecessors – and even by their own commitments.

Changes in exchange parities and in exchange controls are economic events. But they frequently reflect rapid expansions of national money supplies, which ultimately have political explanations.

The firm engaged in international business must recognise these changes in its financial planning. Its day-to-day business transactions – exports and imports, foreign loans and credits, and investments – cause continual changes in its exposure to exchange risk and to political risk. The firm can alter its exposure to these risks if it is willing to pay someone to lend in a foreign currency or to sell a forward contract. The prices attached to assets denominated in several currencies, including forward exchange contracts, vary in response to new information about possible changes in exchange rates and in exchange controls. Competition among investors should cause the prices of both domestic and foreign assets and the exchange rates to change until each asset with its associated risks is willingly held.

Each firm has access to much the same information about the likelihood of changes in exchange rates and exchange controls and their magnitude. Each firm competes with others in its industry in production and marketing; each must decide how its competitive position and its income, net worth, and market value will be affected if it remains exposed to exchange gains and losses.

The modern theory of finance, which provides insights about how investors should develop portfolios of risky assets, can be applied to the firm with international business activities; the firm's exposure in each currency is comparable to the holding of a risky asset by an individual investor. The firm can choose to avoid all exposure to exchange risk and political risk, much like a strongly risk-averse firm of the previous chapter; the analogy is an investor with a completely riskless portfolio. In formulating a strategy towards exposure, the managers must decide whether the firm should arrange the currency mix of its assets and liabilities so as to avoid large variations in income from exchange losses and gains, perhaps at the possible cost of raising its interest expense; or whether instead it should arrange the currency mix so as to profit from anticipated changes in exchange rates.[1] A second question involves the risk – return trade-off available to the firm with assets and liabilities denominated in various foreign currencies both in the short run and in the long run and under alternative exchange rate regimes.

UNCERTAINTY, THE MANAGERS AND THE SHARE-HOLDERS

Modern portfolio theory incorporates uncertainty into investor decisions in a formal way.[2] This theory is structured around two-parameter models of risk and return. The central assumption of this theory is that the investor is risk-averse, and can choose between riskless assets, whose future income is certain, and risky assets, whose future income is uncertain. Each investor seeks to maximise his expected return for a given level of risk – each seeks to minimise his risk for a given expected return. In this context the expected return on each asset is the mean of a distribution of possible returns, each of which has its own probability; the expected return attached to each equity is the dividend and the anticipated change in its price over the relevant investment horizon. The absolute risk of each asset is the variance of the expected return about its mean. Risk and uncertainty are virtually synonymous; if the investor were certain about the future returns he would not be subject to risk.

Competition among investors causes the anticipated returns on the risky assets to exceed those on riskless assets; because investors demand a premium to compensate for holding assets whose future income is uncertain; otherwise no one would hold the risky assets. Similarly, the anticipated returns on assets which are deemed highly risky necessarily exceed those on less risky assets.

One component of this theory is that there are no bargains in the markets for assets – the prices of assets adjust rapidly to new information about prospective changes in their returns. Indeed, as new information becomes available that may affect anticipated returns on an asset, its price immediately moves to the level consistent with prices of other assets with similar return–risk characteristics.

Each investor is concerned with the risk and return of his total portfolio; each relates the risk and return of individual assets to the total risk and return of his portfolio. The investor seeks to maximise the return on his portfolio relative to its risk, where the return is the weighted average of the returns on the securities in the portfolio, and the risk is the variation in the return about its expected level. The risk of a portfolio which includes several assets is smaller than the risk of a portfolio which includes only one of these assets, as long as the variations in the returns of the several assets are not perfectly correlated (if the returns on the two securities are perfectly correlated, the securities are in effect identical). The investor selects individual assets to add to his portfolio because of their contribution to increasing its return and reducing its risk; the risk of the portfolio is smaller than the weighted average of the risks of the securities in the portfolio.

The most efficient portfolio for the investor is the one with the most attractive combination of risk and return. The substitution of one security for another in the portfolio could then not increase its return without increasing its risk, or decrease its risk without reducing its return. There are two distinct steps in using portfolio theory to attain such a portfolio. The first involves estimating the risk–return characteristics of various securities, while the second involves combining these securities into the efficient portfolio.

This model of investor behaviour under uncertainty can be applied to the firm which might acquire assets and liabilities denominated in one or several foreign currencies as a way to reduce its economic exposure. The counterparts of the riskless asset are assets and liabilities denominated in the domestic currency of the firm; the counterpart of the risky asset is a short or long exposure, in a foreign currency. The anticipated return for the firm with net assets or liability denominated in a foreign currency is the sum of the cumulative interest agio and the anticipated change in the foreign currency price of the dollar during the relevant investment period. The risk associated with each equity is the covariance of the expected return with the mean return of the portfolio, while the risk associated with each foreign exchange exposure is the covariance of the expected return in the particular foreign currency asset or liability with the mean return of the portfolio.[3]

The risk of the portfolio of foreign currencies for the firm is smaller than the weighted average of the risks in the individual foreign currencies. There are two distinct steps to determining the firm's exposure in various currencies. The first involves estimating the return and risk parameters for each of the possible foreign currency exposures that the firm might acquire; at issue is whether the firm anticipates deviations from Fisher Open. The second involves combining these exposures in various foreign currencies to obtain the most efficient portfolio of assets and liabilities denominated in various foreign currencies.

As the firm contemplates acquiring a particular asset or liability denominated in a foreign currency, it must determine the contribution of the asset or liability both to the return and to the risk of its portfolio. Hence an exchange rate forecast is a necessary input to determining the anticipated return on this asset or liability.

The returns attached to holding assets and liabilities denominated in several foreign currencies, especially those of the countries in Western Europe that comprise the mark area, are partially correlated, especially in the short run, in that the changes in exchange rates of these currencies relative to the dollar are positively correlated. In general, however, the returns attached to exposures in most foreign currencies appear not to be significantly correlated; changes in the price of the U.S. dollar in terms of most foreign currencies do not occur together. Thus the depreciations of the currencies of most Latin American countries appear unrelated to each other and to the depreciations of the currencies of countries elsewhere.

One theme from the modern theory of finance is that the firm should concentrate on acquiring those investments that maximise its expected return for a given level of risk, and ignore the uncertainty attached to individual investments if costs are attached to dampening the swings in income. The individual investor who is concerned with stabilising his income could avoid the equities of firms whose incomes might vary significantly because of occasional large gains and losses; he could combine securities of firms in different industries to reduce the variance in his own income from sharp variations in the incomes of individual firms.

One implication of this dichotomy between the interests of the firm and the interests of the individual investor is that the firm should not be concerned with the uncertainty about exchange rate changes, but rather it should choose that currency mix of assets and liabilities that maximises its present value. Each firm would have a straightforward decision rule in deciding on its exposure in a particular currency; it would decide whether the interest agio is an upward- or a downward-biased estimate of anticipated changes in exchange rates. If the interest agio is believed to be an upward-biased estimate, the firm would develop a long position in the weak currency, and conversely. Even though the future is uncertain, the firm would make its calculations on the basis of the most likely values for these parameters.

A less extreme version is that the firm would seek to stabilise the level of risk – the variations in its income from changes in exchange rates. The interdependence between variations in income caused by exchange rate changes with variations in income resulting from other factors would be recognised in the selection of domestic assets, and in the size of exposures in individual foreign currencies.

While investors might choose a portfolio of securities, including those of firms subject to large exchange losses and gains, they may shy from the securities of firms with large foreign exchange exposures. The question is whether the firm or individual investors can do a more effective job of diversifying against exchange risk and political risk – and relating these risks to various business risks incurred by the firm. The firm may have superior knowledge, and may be able to protect itself against these risks at lower costs.

The managers of most firms recognise uncertainty in formulating their business decisions, including the size of their exposure in various foreign currencies, perhaps because they believe their shareholders' interests are served by insulating their firms from large variations in income arising from exchange rate gains and losses. Moreover, the managers' personal interests may be advanced by limiting their firm's foreign currency exposure, apparently because they cannot convince individual investors that the firm's interests would be served if it maintained a substantial exposure to enhance its aggregate income, even at the cost of occasional exchange losses. The managers may be concerned that occasional losses incurred from maintaining an exposed position would weigh more heavily against their long-term performance and career prospects than the higher long-run level of income associated with maintaining an exposed position.

If the managers focus solely on maximising the expected return of the firm, the variability of its income will be higher, and so will the risk of bankruptcy. In the textbook world, resources are fungible, established firms fail and new firms are established, and anonymous managers move readily to new firms; failure has no impact on their careers. The less fungible resources are among firms, the larger the concern that individual managers have in preventing sharp swings in the incomes of the firms with which they are associated. Few managers are likely to accept the argument that they should adopt the exposures that will maximise the firm's income in the long run if the implication is that they must occasionally report very large exchange losses.

THE ECONOMIC VIEW OF EXCHANGE RISK

The implication of portfolio theory is that the firm should focus on the risk of its 'portfolio' of exposures in various foreign currencies. In deciding on its exposure in particular currencies, the firm should recognise that most changes in exchange rates, especially of the major currencies, are less than perfectly correlated.[4] The inference from portfolio theory is that risk of the portfolio is smaller than the risks of the individual currencies that comprise the portfolio. Yet for most firms, the decision about whether to develop an exposure in a particular currency arises only if the firm does business in a particular foreign country. And most firms do business in only a small number of foreign countries. Consequently, estimating the risk and return of exposures in foreign currencies is relatively more demanding than optimising a portfolio of such exposures.

The theme of this book is that Fisher Open and Purchasing Power Parity are central to the assessment of risk in international financial markets. If these proportionality propositions adequately describe the empirical relationships among assets and liabilities denominated in various currencies in the short run and in the long run, exchange losses and gains would equal the cumulative interest agio. Regardless of the currency mix of the firm's assets and liabilities, its income, net worth, and presumably its market value would not be affected by changes in the exchange rates. The firm would not be subject to risk if the realised returns could not differ from the expected returns. These propositions provide a useful benchmark for assessment of risk; however, if they fully described the financial world, books on exchange risk would soon be redundant.

A major conclusion of Part I of this book is that the data are not inconsistent with the view that Fisher Open and Purchasing Power Parity are valid propositions in the long run. Over a period of three or four years or longer, the deviations from these propositions average to no more than 2 percentage points a year. In the long run the firm is unlikely to make an expensive mistake about its exposure as long as the deviations from these propositions become no larger. In the short run, however, the interest agio and the forward exchange rate are not precise indicators of the exchange rates that will prevail on the dates when the money market investments and the forward contracts mature. The forecast errors between the 'predicted' exchange rates inferred from the interest agios and the exchange agios, and the observed rates when the predictions mature, appear random rather than systematic. Taken together, these two statements imply that the firm is not significantly exposed in the long run, regardless of the currency mix of its assets and liabilities, and the firm cannot significantly increase its profits by trying to predict changes in exchange rates in the short run.

The firm – and its managers – must decide whether to act on the presumption that the proportionality propositions will remain valid. Even if the conclusion is accepted that the propositions have not been proven invalid in the last 15 or 20 years, the managers cannot be confident that the propositions will prove valid in the future. The managers must decide whether, in the long run, the firm should be indifferent about the currency mix of its assets and liabilities, and how best to adjust to the large short-run deviations from these propositions.

The managers are necessarily concerned with both the firm's accounting exposure and its economic exposure, and the relationship between these two exposures, both in terms of the balance sheet and in terms of the income statement. The major problem becomes how to reconcile the accounting exposure of the firm in the short run with the presumption that the proportionality propositions are likely to hold in the long run. The firm is exposed in accounting terms whenever the sum of assets to be translated at the current exchange rate differs from the sum of liabilities to be translated at this rate. Moreover the domestic value of foreign income would almost certainly be affected by changes in exchange rates. Arranging the currency mix of assets and liabilities denominated in foreign currencies so that the domestic value of foreign income will not be affected by changes in exchange rates means the firm must maintain an accounting exposure.

The firm is exposed in economic terms if, given the currency mix of its assets and liabilities, changes in exchange rates will alter its income. Even though the proportionality propositions are accepted as valid in the long run, the firm's income may vary sharply as a result of exchange gains and losses if the assets and liabilities do not match by currency, and changes in exchange rates occur. Consequently the firm might decide whether to minimise the mismatch of assets and liabilities by currency so as to reduce the cyclical volatility of accounting income. The firm, however, faces a conundrum, for if its foreign subsidiaries own plant and equipment, and the currency mix of assets and liabilities is structured so that it will not have an economic exposure, the value of monetary liabilities denominated in the foreign currencies will exceed the value of monetary assets denominated in these currencies by an amount equal to the value of plant and equipment and inventories. Hence the firm will have an accounting exposure if it seeks to avoid an economic exposure.

Similarly, since the domestic value of foreign income may be affected by changes in exchange rates, the firm may need to arrange the currency mix of its assets and liabilities so as to minimise variations in income that result from changes in exchange rates. The firm would be exposed in accounting terms, since assets and liabilities would not match by currency, but changes in exchange rates would have a smaller impact in causing variations in the time path of reported income.

The managers might adopt one of several different postures towards the exposure problem. One is to count on the validity of the proportionality propositions in the long run, and ignore the short-run variations in accounting income that result from exchange gains and losses. A second is to arrange the currency mix of the firm's assets and liabilities so as to minimise the short-term variations in its reported income resulting from changes in exchange rates. A third is to arrange the currency mix of the firm's assets and liabilities to profit from the apparent modest deviations from the proportionality proposition in the long run, even, perhaps, at the risk of increasing the short-term swings in income as a result of changes in exchange rates. A fourth would involve arranging the currency mix of the firm's assets and liabilities to take advantage of the apparent modest deviations from the proportionality propositions in the long run and, during shorter-run intervals, to seek to profit from the changes in exchange rates in the belief that the exchange agio and the interest agio frequently 'underpredict' sharp swings in exchange rates.

If the managers believe that the proportionality propositions will continue to hold in the long run, they might ignore the currency mix of the firm's assets and liabilities, and concentrate on production and marketing. They would not seek to alter the currency mix of assets and liabilities in anticipation of changes in the exchange rates in the belief that the interest agio and exchange agio would fully reflect the best estimated of these anticipated changes. During some intervals, which include those period when changes in exchange rates are severe, the exchange losses may exceed the cumulative interest agio; during other periods, when changes in exchange rates are modest, the cumulative interest agio would be larger than any exchange losses. As long as the currency mix of the firm's assets and liabilities remains largely unchanged through time, they would believe that its market value and net worth would not be affected by changes in the exchange rate, regardless of the currency mix of its assets and liabilities, despite the occasional large exchange gains at some times and the large losses at other times.

If instead the managers believe that the firm's market value and net worth would be affected by the sequence of large exchange gains and losses, the managers might seek to minimise these variations in income, and the costs of management time and involvement and distraction by maintaining a currency mix of assets and liabilities which has only minimal accounting exposure.[5] The currency mix of assets and liabilities would be managed to minimise the variations in reported income from changes in exchange rates. That Fisher Open is not invalid in the long run means that the firm incurs no cost – and forgoes no income – in the long run by maintaining this currency mix of monetary assets and liabilities which minimises the variations in accounting income. As a consequence, the firm would have an economic exposure in the short run. Yet the firm would not be obliged to allocate substantial resources both to estimating whether particular currencies are likely to appreciate or depreciate and to optimising its portfolio. This approach appears less expensive for the risk-averse firm than continually altering its exposure in response to new information.

A somewhat more ambitious approach would involve attempting to profit from the apparent persistent deviations between the interest rate differentials on long-term securities denominated in different currencies and changes in exchange rates. For example, interest rates in Great Britain and Canada seem high relative to interest rates in the United States even after adjustment for changes in exchange rates. Hence the firm with business activities in either foreign country may seek to profit from these deviations, and develop a long position in these foreign currencies. Thus the firm would seek to increase its income by increasing its borrowing in the currencies in which interest rates appear to be a downward-biased estimate of exchange rate changes, and increasing its lending in those currencies in which the interest rates appear to be an upward-biased estimate of exchange rate changes.[6] The firm would not attempt to predict changes in exchange rates in the short run. Even if this strategy should prove successful, so that the firm's income might be higher in the long run, the variability of its income would also be greater, because changes in exchange rates would result in larger exchange losses and exchange gains.

An even more ambitious approach towards exchange risk would involve altering the currency mix of the firm's assets and liabilities to profit from anticipated short-run deviations between the exchange agio, and the interest agio and changes in exchange rates.[7] If the firm believes that a significant change in the exchange rate is unlikely, then it would arrange the currency mix of its assets and liabilities to minimise its interest payments. As the likelihood of a significant change in the exchange rate appears larger, the firm would increase its long position in strong currency – or reduce its short position in the weak currency, on the presumption that the interest agio almost always underestimates sharp changes in exchange rates. As long as the changes in the exchange rates are modest, the increase in the firm's income would arise from the reduction in its interest payments. In periods when exchange rates change sharply, the increase in the firm's income would arise from the exchange gains – if it had successfully predicted the change. The rationale for this approach is that the interest agio and the exchange agio almost always underpredict sharp changes in exchange rates. This *ex post* inference leaves unsettled, however, how the managers will determine when to alter the currency mix of assets and liabilities.

Increasing the firm's exposure in strong currencies in anticipation that they will appreciate incurs the risk that the expected change in the exchange rate will not occur and that the anticipated exchange gain will not be realised. In a system of pegged exchange rate, this risk appears small – and many currencies are still pegged. The risk is much larger with floating rates, for the data suggest that it is hard to profit from the predictions of changes in exchange rates.

Once the firm decides to attempt to enhance its income by anticipating changes in exchange rates, it must decide when to alter its exposure, the length of the period for which its exposure should be changed, and the size of the change in its exposed position. The firm can anticipate the exchange gains and the cumulative interest agio for intervals of varying lengths, both for those that begin currently and those that begin at various future dates. The more specific the firm attempts to be in estimating the interval in which the change in the exchange rate may occur, the greater the risk.

Many firms have business operations in a substantial number of countries and so may be able to develop portfolios of exposures in various national currencies. Changes in the foreign exchange values of most currencies, with the exception of those in the mark area, and in other currency areas, are not perfectly correlated. The large the number of countries in which the firm is involved, the more diversified its total exposure, and the smaller the impact of unanticipated changes in the exchange rates on the variations in its total income. A firm with an array of exposures in various currencies might conclude that the exchange losses and gains would have a very modest impact on the variability of its total income and so its emphasis should be to minimise its interest costs.

The firm reports its profits on a quarterly and a yearly basis, which is short relative to the period it is involved in most foreign countries. The longer the period in which it can view its exposure, the smaller the risk, and the stronger the case for arranging its exposures to minimise its interest costs.

SUMMARY

The firm with foreign exchange exposures can be viewed as having an analogous position to the investor in the equity market. The firm can remain continually non-exposed, which is equivalent to holding only riskless assets. The exposure in each foreign currency can be viewed as owning a risky asset. As long as changes in various exchange rates are not completely correlated, the firm reduces the riskiness of its portfolio by holding assets and liabilities denominated in various foreign currencies.

In contemplating its exposures in various currencies, the firm must decide on its confidence in Fisher Open as a systematic central tendency, and whether, if Fisher holds, there are non-random biases from Fisher. If the managers believe that Fisher Open holds, they can ignore the firm's exposure, as long as it remains unchanged.

Bibliography

Chapter 2: Changes in Exchange Rates as Economic Disturbances

For a readable introduction to the foreign exchange market see Alan R.
Holmes and Francis H. Schott, *The New York Foreign Exchange
Market* (Federal Reserve Bank of New York, 1965). The evolution of
the system is described in many volumes, including Fred Hirsch, *Money
International* (Harmondsworth: Penguin Books, 1967), Herbert G.
Grubel, *The World Monetary System* (Harmondsworth: Penguin
Books, 1969) and Robert Z. Aliber, *The International Money Game*
(London: Macmillan, 1976). Data on exchange rates, money supply
growth, balance of payments and international reserves are available in
International Monetary Fund, *International Financial Statistics*. Each
year the Fund publishes a comprehensive study, 'The Annual Report on
Exchange Restrictions', which details changes in the barriers to free
international payments. Both the International Monetary Fund in
Washington and the Bank for International Settlements in Basle publish
annual reports detailing changes in institutional payment arrangements
and developments in the international economy. *International Economic
Indicators*, published quarterly by the U.S. Department of Commerce,
presents various data which are useful in determining how each
country's international competitive position is changing. *Economic
Outlook*, published by the Organisation for Economic Co-operation
and Development in Paris, surveys major economic disturbances among
its members.

Chapter 3: Exchange Risk and Yield Differentials

There are numberous studies of the Quantity Theory of Money and its
application in various countries, several on Purchasing Power Parity
and Interest Rate Parity and a few on the Fisher effects. For a
comprehensive analysis of Purchasing Power Parity see Lawrence H.
Officer, 'The Purchasing Power Parity Theory of Exchange Rates: A

141

Review Article', *Staff Papers* (Mar 1976). For a survey of Interest Rate Parity see Lawrence H. Officer and Thomas O. Willet. 'The Covered Arbitrage Schedule: A Critical Survey of Recent Developments', *Journal of Money, Credit and Banking* (May 1970) and Robert Z. Aliber, 'The Interest Rate Parity Theory: A Reinterpretation', *Journal of Political Economy* (Nov–Dec 1973).

Chapter 4: Political Risk and the International Investment

For some conceptual material see Dan Haendel and Gerald T. West with Robert G. Meadow, 'Overseas Investment and Political Risk', Foreign Policy Research Institute Monograph Series (Nov 1975). For a description of the external currency market see Robert Z. Aliber, 'The Impact of External Markets for National Currencies or Central Bank Reserves', in Harry G. Johnson and Alexander K. Swoboda (eds.), *The Economics of Common Currencies* (London: Allen and Unwin, 1973).

Chapter 5: Changes in Exchange Rates and National Commodity Price Levels

One study on the empirical context of Purchasing Power Parity is B. Balassa, 'The Purchasing Power Parity Doctrine: A Reappraisal', *Journal of Political Economy* (Dec 1964), reprinted in R. N. Cooper, *Readings in International Finance* (Harmondsworth: Penguin Books, 1969). See also Henry J. Gaillot, 'Purchasing Power Parity as an Explanation of Long-Term Changes in Exchange Rates', *Journal of Money, Credit and Banking* (Aug 1970) and Richard J. Rogalski and Joseph D. Vinso, 'Price Level Variations as Predictors of Flexible Exchange Rates', *Journal of International Business Studies* (Spring–Summer 1977).

Chapter 6: Changes in Exchange Rates and Yield Differentials

Within the last several years a number of studies have questioned whether the forward exchange rates and the interest rate differentials are unbiased predictors of future spot exchange rates. These studies include Richard M. Levich, 'The International Money Market: Tests of Forecasting Models and Market Efficiency', unpublished Ph.D. dissertation (University of Chicago, 1977); John F. O. Bilson and Richard M. Levich, 'A Test of the Forecasting Efficiency of the Forward Exchange Rate' (Graduate School of Business Administration, New York University No. 77–61, June 1977); David L. Kaserman, 'The Forward Rate: Its Determination and Behavior as a Predictor of the Future Spot Exchange Rate', *Proceedings of the American Statistical Association* (1973); Steven W. Kohlhagen, 'The Forward Rate as an Unbiased Prediction of the Future Spot Rate', mimeo (Berkeley: University of California, 1974). For tests of Fisher Open on longer term securities see Michael G. Porter, 'A Theoretical and Empirical Framework for Analyzing the Term Structures of Exchange Rate Expectations', *Staff Papers* (Nov 1971), and Ronald Moses, 'Anticipations of Exchange Rate Changes', Ph.D. dissertation (University of Chicago, 1969). For the analysis of whether day-to-day and week-to-week movements in exchange rates are systematic or random see Ian Giddy and Gunter Dufey, 'The Random Behavior of Flexible Exchange Rates', *Journal of International Business Studies* (Spring 1975); Michael P. Dooley and Jeffrey R. Shafer, 'Analysis of Short-Run Exchange Rate Behavior, March 1975 to September 1975', Working Paper 76 (Board of Governors, Federal Reserve System, 1977); William Poole, 'The Canadian Experiment with Flexible Exchange Rates', Ph.D. dissertation (University of Chicago, 1966), and his 'Speculative Prices on Random Walks: An Analysis of Ten Time Series of Flexible Exchange Rates', *Southern Economical Journal* (Apr 1967).

Chapter 7: Interest Rate Differentials and Political Risk

There appear to be no data-oriented studies on deviations from Interest Rate Parity across currencies or deviations between onshore and offshore interest rates for currencies other than the dollar. See Richard J. Herring and Richard C. Marston, *National Monetary Policies and International Financial Markets* (Amsterdam: North-Holland, 1977) esp. chap. 4.

Chapter 8: The Costs of Altering Exposure to Exchange Risk

A member of texts and monographs describe the techniques for altering exposure to exchange risk. See David K. Eteman and Arthur I. Stonehill, *International Business Finance* (Reading, Mass.: Addison-

Wesley, 1973) chap. 11, and/or J. Fred Weston and Bart W. Sorge, *International Managerial Finance* (Homewood, Ill.: Irwin, 1972) chap. 5. Few materials deal correctly with the cost of altering exposure to exchange risk; one which does is Business International, 'Hedging Foreign Exchange Risks', Management Monograph No. 99 (1971).

Chapter 9: Exchange Exposure in a Multiple Currency World

Within the last several years the number of articles on accounting aspects of exchange risk has increased, both because of the move to floating exchange rates and because of the Federal Accounting Standards Board's 'Accounting for the Translation of Foreign Currency Transactions and Foreign Currency Financial Statements into Dollars'. See Leonard Lorensen, *Reporting Foreign Operations of U.S. Companies in Dollars*, Accounting Research Study No. 12 (New York: American Institute of Certified Public Accountants, 1972). For earlier views see Donald J. Hays, 'Translating Foreign Currencies', *Harvard Business Review* (Jan–Feb 1972) and Marvin M. Deupree, 'Translating Foreign Currency Financial Statements to U.S. Dollars', *Financial Executive* (Oct 1972).

Chapter 10: Tax Implications of Exchange Losses and Gains

The classic on the tax aspects is Donald R. Ravenscroft, *Taxation and Foreign Spending* (Cambridge, Mass.: Harvard University Law School, 1973). See also Peggy B. Musgrave, 'Exchange Rate Aspects in the Taxation of Foreign Income', *National Tax Journal* (Dec 1975); also John J. Costello, 'Tax Consequences of Speculation and Hedging in Foreign Currency Futures', *Tax Lawyer* (Winter 1975) and his 'Tax Impact of Currency Exchange Rate Fluctuations', *Tax Lawyer* (Spring 1973).

Chapter 11: Strategies Towards Exchange Risk

There are numerous sources of advice on strategy, including Gunter Dufey, 'Corporate Finance and Exchange Rate Variations', *Financial Management* (Summer 1972). For management science approaches see Bernard A. Lietaer, 'Managing Risks in Foreign Exchange', *Harvard*

Business Review (Mar–Apr 1970), which is largely abstracted from his book *Financial Management of Foreign Exchange* (Cambridge, Mass.: MIT Press, 1971). Other management science approaches include David Ruttenberg, 'Maneuvering Liquid Assets in a Multinational Corporation', *Management Science* (June 1970), and Alan C. Shapiro, 'Hedging Against Devaluations: A Management Science Approach', in C. G. Alexander (ed.), *International Business Systems Perspectives* (Georgia State University, 1973). For a very different approach see Robert B. Shulman, 'Are Foreign Exchange Risks Measurable', *Columbia Journal of World Business* (May–June 1970); also John T. Wooster and G. Richard Thomas, 'New Financial Priorities for MNC', *Harvard Business Review* (May–June 1974).

Notes

1. In this monograph the U.S. dollar is the numeraire currency. Hence all exchange rates involve a statement of the number of local currency units per U.S. dollar. Devaluation and depreciation mean that the number of units of foreign currency required to buy one dollar increases; revaluation and appreciation mean that the number of foreign currency units declines. For the treasurer of a U.S. firm the dollar is never devalued or revalued; the dollar never appreciates or depreciates.

An alternative approach states the number of U.S. currency units required to buy the foreign unit, which is consistent with the way most commodity prices are quoted. But unnecessary confusion would result because Americans would state the number of cents (dollars) per mark, while Germans would state the number of marks per dollar.

CHAPTER 2

1. The terms used to describe exchange rate systems are ambiguous. 'Floating', 'flexible' and 'fluctuating' are all used to describe a floating rate, while the term 'fixed rate' has been used to describe what might better be called a 'pegged rate' or an 'adjustable parity'. 'Flexible rate' is a generic term at the same level of generality as 'fixed rate'; 'floating rates', 'pegged rates' and 'adjustable parities' are specific types of flexible systems.

2. As part of monetary reform arrangements incorporated in the Smithsonian Agreement in December 1971 some countries dropped the term 'parity' and substituted 'central rate'.

3. Very large devaluations almost always occur after a country has adopted extensive controls. The large change reflects substantial overvaluation; without controls, individuals and firms would have shifted funds abroad to profit from the anticipated change in the exchange rate.

4. The distinction between international money and domestic money is discussed on pp. 15–16.

5. If countries follow dependent monetary policies, then changes in price levels are required to achieve payments balance at the existing parity levels. If, instead, countries follow independent monetary policies, then changes in exchange rates are necessary to achieve payments balance at the prevailing price levels.

6. Most of the oil-producing countries did not revalue following the sharp increase in their export earnings as a result of the increase in the price of crude petroleum. These surpluses have led to a sharp increase in government revenues,

but some of the governments hold much of their financial assets abroad, so their domestic money supplies are not directly affected by their payments surpluses.

7. In a two-country, two-currency world, only one of the central banks need peg its currency for the 'exchange rate system' to be pegged. In an N-currency world, only $N-1$ central banks need peg their currencies for all currencies to be pegged.

8. Devaluations tend to reduce wages and increase profits, at least in the short run; revaluations, in contrast, tend to reduce profits and increase wages. The permanence of such changes in the distribution of income depends on the subsequent domestic monetary policies.

9. With the breakdown of the Bretton Woods system and the Smithsonian Agreement, the system lacks rules to constrain the behaviour of central banks in the exchange market.

CHAPTER 3

1. The relative version is used most frequently in economic analysis, since it can be applied using readily available price indexes. In contrast, testing the absolute version requires extensive collection of actual prices for many goods in both countries. Moreover, since the exchange rate may be affected by non-commodity transactions, such as military expenditures and capital flows, the absolute version may not indicate the equilibrium exchange rate.

2. The relative version of Purchasing Power Parity can be expressed in terms of levels of the price ratios and of the exchange rate as well, as in the text, in terms of the rates of change. The text follows the latter approach for consistency with other proportionality propositions.

3. These deviations from Purchasing Power Parity might be larger, the more rapid the rate of domestic economic growth. Rapid growth may be associated with a sharp increase in export competitiveness, and with a growing spread between changes in export prices and changes in prices of goods and services which are not traded internationally.

4. Note that if the price level relationship in the diagram is shown in terms of the level of the ratio, each episode of structural change leads to a permanent shift in the *PPP* function. When the price level relationship is shown in terms of rate of change, the *PPP* function shifts only as long as the structural change continues.

5. These propositions, named after Irving Fisher, focus on the relationships between changes in commodity price levels, changes in money interest rates and changes in exchange rates. *The Theory of Interest* (New York: Macmillan, 1930).

6. The equivalence between Purchasing Power Parity and Fisher Open means that Purchasing Power Parity is expressed in terms of annual rates of change, while the interest agio is expressed in terms of differences in the interest rates on domestic and foreign securities.

7. Some forward contracts permit the holder to select the date of maturity within a certain range of dates.

8. The Interest Rate Parity Theorem is sometimes confused with the Fisher Open. The concepts are distinct; Fisher Open states that the differential in interest rates on similar assets denominated in different currencies depends on

the anticipated change in the exchange rate, while the Interest Rate Parity Theorem states that the forward exchange rate on contracts negotiated today depends on the interest agio. For a variety of institutional reasons, including investor concern with political risk, the forward rate may differ from the anticipated exchange rate.

9. For expositional ease, the interest agio is written $r_d - r_f$.

10. Confusion sometimes arises about whether domestic currency is at a forward discount, especially when the exchange rate is quoted as the number of foreign currency units per U.S. dollar. Thus if the forward pengo is 4.02 per dollar and the spot pengo is 4.00 per dollar, the pengo is at a forward discount, since more pengos are required to buy the dollar in the forward market than in the spot market.

11. The implicit assumption is that the investor based in New York computes his net worth in dollars, while the investor based in Ruthenia computes his net worth in pengos.

12. Political risk is discussed in the next chapter.

13. Note that the monetary disturbance leads to deviations from Purchasing Power Parity, for the exchange rate predicted by changes in Ruthenian prices relative to world prices should approximate that in the Fisherian model.

14. Note that the equivalence between Purchasing Power Parity and Fisher Open means that Purchasing Power Parity is expressed in terms of annual rates of change, while the interest agio is expressed in terms of differences in the interest rates on domestic and foreign securities.

15. In a two-currency, dollar–mark world, there is no indication of whether the currency premium should be in favour of the mark or the dollar. One analogy of a possible currency premium in the foreign exchange market is the 'backwardation premium' in the commodity markets – future prices are said to be downward-biased estimates of spot prices on the maturity of future contracts because hedgers must pay speculators to carry uncertainty. A second analogy is the Keynesian-type liquidity premium in the bond market; interest rates on long-term bonds are said to be higher than interest rates on shorter-term securities in the same risk class because investors demand a payment for bearing the risk of larger adverse price swings. The relevance of both analogies is questionable, however, because the 'trades' in the foreign exchange market involve two moneys rather than a money and a commodity, or a money and an interest-bearing asset.

CHAPTER 4

1. Whereas exchange risk centres on possible changes in a price variable – the exchange rate – political risk involves possible changes in quantity variables, exchange controls. Changes in exchange controls have consequences on asset prices.

2. In the Euro-bond market, borrowers issue securities denominated in currencies other than that of the country in which they are located. Thus, U.S. and German firms have issued mark-denominated bonds in London and Luxembourg; these bonds share the exchange risk attribute of mark bonds issued in Germany but not their political risk attribute. The growth of the Euro-

bond market was a response to the U.S. Interest Equalisation Tax (IET), which raised the cost to foreign borrowers of issuing dollar securities in the United States. Before the IET some foreign borrowers found it cheaper to issue dollar securities in New York than securities in their domestic markets denominated in their domestic currencies. The foreign borrowers responded to the IET by issuing dollar securities outside the United States; these securities were purchased by lenders who had a preference for dollar-denominated securities and were not greatly concerned about whether the securities were issued in New York or London. Subsequently, borrowers used the market to reduce interest costs by issuing securities in centres which did not apply a withholding tax to the payment of interest.

3. The U.S. authorities regulate the foreign activities of U.S. firms and foreign branches of U.S. banks, although not on the same terms. Such regulations might be more restrictive than those of the host governments; they cannot be effective and yet be less restrictive, unless these branches are prepared to ignore the regulations of countries in which they are located. But the U.S. authorities cannot regulate the activities of non-U.S. banks in London and in Singapore that produce dollar assets, nor can they control the use of the dollar as unit-of-account by foreign nationals.

4. Regulation of financial transactions imposes costs, so that either lenders receive a lower interest income or borrowers pay higher interest charges.

5. The assumption in this analysis is that commercial banks 'produce' demand deposits and time deposits. The ability of an individual bank to grow is determined by its ability to sell deposits to firms and individuals. Traditionally, banks in the United States produced deposits denominated in dollars, while banks in Great Britain produced deposits denominated in sterling.

6. For data on the volume of external currency deposits denominated in various currencies, see Bank for International Settlements, *Annual Reports*, for various years.

7. These comparisons implicitly assume that it is as easy to shift funds from New York to London to acquire dollar deposits as it is to acquire deposits denominated in sterling.

8. A useful analogy to offshore banks is provided by domestic savings and loan associations and building societies, which seek to attract deposits from commercial banks by offering owners of deposits higher interest rates than those paid by the banks. Whenever they sell a deposit or a share, they receive in exchange a cheque representing ownership of a deposit in a bank. Offshore banks sell deposits in exchange for deposits in domestic banks.

9. Thus the interest differentials between domestic and offshore deposits denominated in the same currency provide an estimate of the marginal investor's assessment of the political risk. Inferences about the riskiness of various offshore centres cannot be based solely on interest differentials, since all offshore interests rates are the same.

10. The relevant data for these statements are discussed in Chapter 7.

11. Political risk is a more complex phenomenon than exchange risk. British investors are concerned that the U.S. authorities might constrain repatriation of funds from New York, while American investors are concerned that the British authorities might constrain repatriation of funds from London.

12. Governments in the industrial countries provide insurance against losses

on foreign investment to promote foreign policy objectives, exports and the income of foreign investors.

CHAPTER 5

1. Even if these propositions are valid, individual firms might conclude that their net worth might be adversely affected by changes in exchange rates; their conclusions reflect the biases in the accounting conventions. The shortcomings in the traditional accounting approaches to the estimation of the exposure to exchange risk are discussed in Chapter 9.

2. Several strategies are discussed in Chapter 11.

3. Some insight into acceptable levels of deviation from Purchasing Power Parity is available in the response of firms to increases in domestic prices. Within a country, firms traditionally ignore changes in the prices of their non-monetary assets in constructing their balance sheets; they value plant and equipment at historical cost, regardless of subsequent changes in the market value of these assets. Implicitly, the firms recognise that the differences between market values and historic costs may not be significant as long as the rate of inflation is less than 3, 5 or even 10 per cent a year. By analogy, a rate of deviation from Purchasing Power Parity of no more than 2 or 3 per cent a year, even on a cumulative basis, might not be so large as to lead firms to reject the concept in their financial planning. The U.S. experience suggests that the rate of inflation might have to approach 10 per cent a year before business pressures towards the adoption of price level accounting as an alternative to historic cost accounting would become substantial.

4. Similar ratios also have been computed using the wholesale price and tradeables price indexes; the deviations based on these price indexes are smaller than those based on the consumer price indexes.

5. Rather than use exchange rate behaviour as the criterion for grouping countries, the changes in the behaviour of the ratio could be used, with those countries for which deviations from either direction are small placed in one group, those with deviations substantially above in a second group, and those with deviations substantially below in a third group.

6. For example, assume the value of the ratio changes from 1.0 to 1.2 as a result of changing the base year. Over a ten-year period the average annual rate of deviation changes by 2.0 per cent; over a twenty-year period, by 1.0 per cent.

1. The interest rates on long-term securities used in this comparison are those on government bonds; the data are from *International Financial Statistics*. Firms are borrowers, not lenders, and so a more meaningful comparison would involve the interest rates paid by the same firm when it borrows in different currencies. The spread between the interest rates on government securities and corporate securities appears smaller in the United States than in most foreign countries,

and so the estimate of deviation from Fisher Open using government securities may understate the deviation on corporate securities.

2. A differential of 2 per cent a year seems unusually large in terms of transactions costs and differences in tax treatment.

3. Some of the additional return on the Canadian dollar bonds might be construed as a premium for political risk. Lenders are concerned that if they acquire Canadian dollar bonds, the repatriation of interest and capital at some future date might be constrained by the regulations of Canadian authorities. They also may be concerned that Canadian securities are somewhat more risky than U.S. securities, perhaps because the markets in which they are traded are thinner and subject to more abrupt price swings.

4. See Chapter 7, for a discussion of whether the interest rate differential on long-term bonds after adjustment for changes in exchange rates is high or low relative to losses investors incur from other factors.

5. The exchange agio is tested by using the interest rate data on Euro-deposits.

6. This conclusion is consistent with the findings of most other investigators. See Richard N. Levich, 'The International Money Market: Tests of Forecasting Models and Market Efficiency', unpublished Ph.D. thesis, University of Chicago, June 1977.

7. In most forecasts the large movements are almost always underpredicted. The explanation is that most forecasts give substantial weight to recent price movements, and the large movements are – by definition – substantial relative to recent price movements.

8. From time to time an observer will report that the error terms are correlated and conclude that the exchange rate does not follow a random walk. Such findings may reflect central bank intervention in the exchange market undertaken to dampen the swings in the spot exchange rate.

9. It is possible that daily data might show that the forward discount overstates changes in the exchange rates in the week or two before the parity changes. Casual observation, however, denies this proposition.

CHAPTER 7

1. Unless the subsidiary is expropriated or goes bankrupt, borrowing within the host country increases its interest costs without reducing its exposure to losses because of arbitrary actions of host-country governments. Thus the petroleum companies in the Middle East were obliged to sell their properties to host governments at prices lower than those they liked; their losses would not have been smaller if they had borrowed more in the host countries. Similarly, altering the source of financing offers minimum protection against losses due to government pricing, licensing and other restrictive arrangements.

2. For data on changes in exchange controls, see Exchange Restrictions, *Annual Report* (Washington: International Monetary Fund).

3. For example, see J. Frederick Truitt, 'Expropriation of Foreign Investment: Summary of the Post-World War II Experience of American and British Investors in Less Developed Countries', *Journal of International Business Studies* (Fall 1970).

4. For example, the interest rates paid by U.S. firms on loans in Canadian

dollars exceed interest rates on U.S. dollar loans by 1 per cent or more, even after an adjustment for the changes in exchange rates. Exchange controls have not yet affected the repatriation of capital from Canada.

5. Estimates of transactions costs on single transactions vary from 0.1 to 0.2 or 0.3 per cent, depending on the foreign currency, whether it is pegged or floating, whether the transaction is in the spot market or in the forward market, and whether the transaction is undertaken by a bank or a commercial firm. Arbitrage transactions involve two transactions, one in the spot market and one in the forward market, and so two transactions costs must be summed.

6. Because the estimates are averages of weekly data, they may obscure large deviations which persist for a few weeks or a few months.

7. With securities which are deemed identical in terms of susceptibility to political risk, such as London dollar deposits and London Swiss franc deposits, most of the deviations from Interest Rate Parity are less than 0.5 per cent.

8. The explanation for this echo effect is that interest rates on offshore deposits denominated in currencies other than the dollar are linked to the interest rates on offshore dollar deposits by forward exchange rates. If the exchange agios remain unchanged as U.S. monetary policy becomes more contractive, then offshore dollar interest rates will rise, and interest rates on offshore deposits denominated in every other currency will increase by the same amount.

9. The relationship is not symmetric, in that a shift to monetary stringency in a country other than the United States has only a modest impact on the offshore dollar rate, since the dollar component accounts for three-quarters of the offshore market, and is more than four times larger than the next largest component, which is the German mark.

CHAPTER 8

1. This view of the riskless position is in nominal terms. While nominal net worth may not be affected by changes in exchange rates if the firm is completely hedged, its net worth in real terms may be affected, since domestic prices, costs and profits will change as the exchange rate changes. In Part II, for expositional ease, the firm's exposure is measured in the foreign currency rather than the dollar.

2. In addition, a variety of government agencies sell 'insurance' against various risks of international business, usually on a subsidised basis, either to achieve a national foreign policy objective or an economic objective. For a description of these government insurance programmes see Marina V. N. Whitman, *Government Risk Sharing in Foreign Investment* (Princeton U.P.: 1965).

3. The cost of altering exposure in this chapter is not identical with the cost of hedging as used by corporate treasurers and bankers; they almost always use the term to mean the interest agio or the exchange agio. In this book the cost of altering exposure is the net of the *change* in the cumulative interest agio or the exchange agio and the *change* in the exchange gain or loss as the currency mix of the firm's assets and liabilities is altered. Because the change in the exchange gain or loss can be known only at the conclusion of the investment period, the cost initially is estimated.

4. Exposure is measured in the foreign currency, although it has a value in the domestic currency at the current exchange rate.

5. This discussion assumes that the firm wishes to hedge an exposure arising from ownership of a pengo asset. Instead the firm might wish to hedge a pengo income stream; the story is identical and the only complication is that change in the exchange rate may affect the size of the income stream in pengos in an uncertain way.

6. Some writers distinguish translation gains and losses from transaction gains and losses on the basis of realisation; translation losses and gains are unrealised. This distinction loses much of its operational significance following the Federal Accounting Standards Board No. 8 recommendation, which requires that both exchange gains and losses be recognised in the quarter in which they occur, regardless of whether they have been realised. See page 105.

7. Changes in exchange rates affect the value of outstanding forward contracts implicitly, if not explicitly, since forward contracts, unlike futures contracts, are not tradeable. Assume a firm had sold sterling forward on a six-month contract on 1 Jan 1977, at a rate of $2.00. Sterling depreciates to $1.75. The implicit value of the contract to receive $2.00 is $2.00 $1.75 or £1.14.

8. The use of commodity futures markets to alter a currency exposure should be distinguished from arbitraging between the commodity futures market in several different countries in anticipation of a change in the exchange rate. Assume an investor has a long position in sterling and believes that sterling may depreciate. He might buy copper futures contracts denominated in sterling in the London market, and sell copper futures denominated in dollars in the New York market, in anticipation that the sterling price of copper will rise as sterling depreciates, so that the value of his London futures contracts will increase. He also believes the dollar price of copper will remain unchanged, so that the dollar price of copper futures contracts will remain unchanged. The combination of the purchase of copper futures in sterling and the sale of copper futures in dollars protects the investor against a price risk. See John R. Dominguez, *Devaluation and Futures Markets* (Lexington, Mass.: D. C. Heath, 1972).

9. An analogy is provided by the anticipated return from holding equity or debt, which is the sum of the dividend or interest receipts and the change in the price of the asset during the holding period. Both must be anticipated. Investors acquire equity and debt only if the anticipated returns are positive. If the price of the asset falls by more than the dividend or interest receipts, the realised returns are negative.

10. Exchange speculation and interest arbitrage occur only if investors anticipate deviations from Fisher Open.

11. The estimate of the cost of hedging in these several paragraphs differs from the more traditional measure, which calculates the cost as $(F-S_t)/S_t$, or the forward discount or premium. The traditional measure usually greatly overestimates the cost of altering exposure. Indeed, to the extent that forward rates are on average unbiased predictors of the spot rates on the maturities of the forward contracts, no cost is attached to altering the firm's exposure.

12. For expository ease it is assumed that no explicit interest rate and no implicit convenience yield are attached to money holdings in the several centres.

13. These several estimates of the costs of altering exposure should be distinguished from the transactions costs associated with hedging. These

transactions costs are usually very low. Moreover, if the firm hedges by using forward contracts, the associated transactions costs are likely to be only modestly larger than those associated with the spot exchange transaction that the firm would otherwise have made.

CHAPTER 9

1. This approach for estimation of exposure to exchange risk can be readily adapted to estimation of exposure to political risk.

2. For expository ease, the term 'domestic currency' is that used by the parent firm in presenting its income statement and balance sheet. The term 'local currency' is that used by the subsidiary in developing its balance sheet within the country in which it is based; most of the items in this balance sheet are denominated in the local currency. The term 'foreign currency' is used for assets or liabilities held by the parent denominated in a currency other than that of the country in which the parent is based.

3. The analysis in this chapter is developed for a U.S. firm with net worth expressed in dollars. Similar analyses might be developed for a British firm with a net worth expressed in sterling, or a Dutch firm with a net worth expressed in guilders. Simple transformations can be used to determine whether the deviations from Purchasing Power Parity and Fisher Open for firms based in other countries are larger or smaller than they are for U.S. firms.

4. The economists are concerned with the costs of altering exposure, whereas the accountants are concerned solely with the exchange losses that might result from changes in exchange rates. The distinction between the approaches of the economists and of the accountants can be highlighted with the metaphor of a fire insurance company. The economists measure the success of the company by looking at the relation between payments to insured on policy claims and the premium income from the insured, while the accountants measure its success by looking only at the payments to the insured.

5. George C. Watt, 'Foreign Exchange Transactions and Translation', in Sidney Davidson and Roman L. Weil (eds.), *Handbook of Modern Accounting* (New York: McGraw-Hill, 1977) ch. 35, p. 26.

6. This discussion assumes that the U.S. parent owns 100 per cent of the shares of the foreign subsidiary. If the U.S. firm holds less than 100 per cent of the shares, its ownership is usually represented by an asset entry in its balance sheet, which is known as the net equity method. Subsequent changes in the foreign exchange value of the currency of the country in which the subsidiary is located require that the value of the investment be translated at the current exchange rate, much as if the parent owns a financial asset denominated in the foreign currency.

7. The use of the current exchange rate for translation implies that the currency is neither seriously overvalued nor undervalued. If payments from subsidiary to parent are severely constrained by the host-country exchange controls, a black market rate may be more appropriate for translation than the current exchange rate.

8. *Accounting Research Bulletin*, No. 43 (New York: American Institute of Certified Public Accountants, 1965) chap. 12.

9. *Accounting Principles Board Opinion No. 6* (New York: American Institute of Certified Public Accountants, 1965).

10. When 'men of affairs' recommend that all assets and liabilities except bricks and mortar be hedged, they imply that the current exchange rate should be used to translate all of the balance-sheet items other than plant and equipment – in effect AICPA II.

11. The Council of the Institute of Chartered Accountants in England and Wales recommends either of two methods of translation, the closing rate and historic rate method. The closing rate method is equivalent to the use of the current exchange rate in the United States. The historic rate approach is most nearly comparable to AICPA I. In 1970 the Research and Publications Committee of the Institute of Chartered Accountants of Scotland stated a preference for the closing rate approach. Most British firms appear to follow the historic approach. See the Institute of Chartered Accountants in England and Wales, *Recommendations on Accounting Principles*, chap. 25. Canadian firms generally follow a distinction between monetary and non-monetary items. See R. MacDonald Parkinson, *Translation of Foreign Currencies* (Canadian Institute of Chartered Accountants, 1972).

12. If the subsidiary incurs a large revaluation gain or loss because of its exposure, and an adjustment may be made in its retained earnings. If the parent incurs a large revaluation gain or loss because of its exposure in its subsidiary, the parent may adjust its retained earnings.

13. Consistency requires that depreciation as well as plant and equipment be translated at the historic exchange rate.

14. See Marvin Deupree, 'Translating Foreign Currency Financial Statements into U.S. Dollars', *Financial Executive* (Oct 1972) pp. 46–8.

15. Prior to the move to a uniform approach, about one-third of U.S. firms followed AICPA I, one-third AICPA II, and the rest a variety of other approaches. See Sidney M. Robbins and Robert B. Stobaugh, *Money in the Multinational Enterprise* (New York: Basic Books, 1973).

16. While revenues and expenses are to be translated at the current exchange rate, as in the pre-FASB approaches, the 'cost of goods' sold is translated at the historic exchange rate, which is consistent with translation of inventories at the historic exchange rate.

17. Financial Accounting Standards Board, *Accounting for Foreign Currency Translation* (Stanford, Conn., 1975).

18. Some firms allocated foreign exchange gains to a reserve, which was then charged when exchange losses were incurred. This approach enabled firms to reduce the impact of translation gains and losses on domestic income. The FASB recommendations mean a reserve account is no longer beneficial. Prior to the FASB recommendations, few if any firms allocated the cumulative interest agio to the reserve account.

19. For example, assume the subsidiary finances the establishment of a foreign subsidiary by borrowing in the host country's currency. That the plant and equipment is translated at the historic rate, and the foreign currency debt at the current rate, indicates that the firm has a short accounting exposure. If Purchasing Power Parity holds, the local currency value of the plant and equipment will increase as the foreign currency depreciates.

20. Numerous firms attributed large exchange losses to FASB No. 8. These

reported accounting losses resulted from the combination of the currency mix of their assets and liabilities and the change in the exchange rates. Most firms could readily have adjusted the currency mix of their assets and liabilities in response to FASB No. 8 so as to have the same post-FASB exposure as before; the required adjustment would almost always have involved a reduction in foreign currency borrowing.

21. Some observers may not believe that the data confirm Purchasing Power Parity and Fisher Open. Acceptance of the economic approach to estimation of exposure is independent of the position taken on the validity of these propositions in the past. Thus, the concepts can be used as benchmarks, and economic exposure estimated as deviations from these benchmarks.

22. Even if Fisher Open should prove valid, the firm might incur an exchange loss if it holds non-interest-bearing financial assets, e.g. receivables or money. An implicit convenience yield is attached to both assets, and the nominal value of this convenience yield increases as the inflation rate increases. The convenience yield is not carried in the profit and loss statement of the firm.

23. See Alfred M. King, 'Budgeting Foreign Exchange Losses', *Management Accounting* (Oct 1969) pp. 39–46.

24. If the interval for estimating exposure is longer than the maturity of the financial assets or liabilities held by the firm, the cumulative interest agio must also be estimated. During some intervals the cumulative interest agio exceeds the percentage change in the exchange rate; about the time of parity changes or when the rate moves sharply under the floating system, the percentage change in the exchange rate is larger.

25. An alternative economic approach to the measurement of exposure involves projections of the impact of changes in exchange rates on the cash flows of the firm. The firm is exposed to the extent that changes in exchange rates cause changes in the domestic value of the these currency flows. Changes in the currency mix of assets and liabilities changes exposure. The shortcoming of this approach is that cash flows are not offset against translation gains and losses.

26. The distortion, if any, caused by this change depends on the turnover period for inventories. The less rapidly inventories turn over, the greater the possible discrepancy between the reported value of inventories and the economic value.

27. Similarly, the shift from AICPA I to AICPA II would have required a one-time adjustment in the firm's net position in foreign currencies for the firm to attain the identical accounting exposure under AICPA II that it had under AICPA I.

28. The one case in which the reduction of the liabilities denominated in a foreign currency would increase the firm's interest payments is for a firm with Swiss franc liabilities.

29. Some firms might believe that the reduction in foreign indebtedness will increase their exposure to loss from expropriation. They believe that if their subsidiary in a particular country is expropriated by a host country, the parent will not be obliged to repay the debt. This proposition, however, obscures the distinction between the currency in which the subsidiary borrows and whether the debts of the subsidiary are guaranteed by the parent. Casual empiricism suggests that the interest savings associated with denominating debt in dollars

rather than in the foreign currency are large relative to the losses from expropriation.

30. Some firms appear reluctant to develop a square position under FASB; they argue that they are now required to hedge a translation exposure. For example, if a firm has a long-term liability denominated in a foreign currency, the firm is required to report an exchange loss when that currency appreciates and an exchange gain when that currency depreciates. The managers may be concerned with the cash flow implication of hedging the translation exposure. They might buy the foreign currency forward; then, when the forward contract matures, they would sell the foreign currency received from settlement of the forward contract in the spot market and at the same time, buy the foreign currency forward once again.

31. The implication of the statement that Fisher Open does not hold is that there are persistent profit opportunities to be made in maintaining a long (short) position.

CHAPTER 10

1. This chapter deals with the economic aspects of the taxation of exchange losses and gains. The assumptions are that the parent firm incurs an exchange loss or gain as a result of a change in exchange rates, while the income of the subsidiary in the host country's currency is unchanged.

2. Hence if the depreciation of the pengo reduces the dollar value of the pengo-denominated monetary assets, while the dollar value of pengo income is unchanged, the firm's tax liability is unchanged, even though its reported U.S. income is reduced because of the exchange loss on the pengo-denominated monetary assets.

3. A subsidiary is incorporated in the foreign country whereas a branch is not incorporated.

4. The U.S. tax authorities determine the tax liability on foreign operations on the basis of the U.S. definition of income, not on the host-country definition.

5. The profit on the forward contract is the difference between the pengo cost of the forward contracts on the date acquired, and the pengo value of the dollars received on the maturity of the forward contract; the pengo profit would be translated into dollars at the current exchange rate.

6. Note that if the forward exchange rate is an unbiased predictor of the future spot exchange rate, the firm earns no profits on its forward contracts. And there is no cost to buying forward contracts, other than the transactions costs. Should the spot rate depreciate by less than the prediction inherent in the forward rate, the firm would incur an exchange loss; usually this loss would reduce its taxable income.

7. The tax treatment of income on forward contracts by the U.S. tax authorities is in flux. Thus, 'to attempt to assume that income from a hedging operation will be considered as capital gains rather than normal income, the forward contract has to run for more than six months, preferably for at least 10 months but still better for one year, and it should be sold one or two months before maturity, preferably to a bank or person other than the original

contractor'. Business International, *Hedging Foreign Exchange Risks*, Management Monograph No. 49 (1971) p. 19.

8. The distinction rests on where the title to the forward contract is transferred, which is probably identical with the location of the bank issuing the contract.

9. The technique discussed in this paragraph involves the shuffling of income similar to that used in the usual examples of transfer-pricing.

CHAPTER 11

1. This position is considered more fully in the next chapter.

2. The risk neutralisation would be judged in relation to the currently accepted accounting recommendations for translation of assets and liabilities denominated in foreign currencies into dollars.

3. Many firms stress that they only hedge their risks – that they never speculate. But this statement cannot be true for firms as a group, given the evidence on the massive swings of funds when the maintenance of the current values for the exchange rates seems unlikely. Many firms reduce or eliminate their exposed positions as the likelihood of changes in exchange rates increases, in the belief that the interest agio or the exchange agio is low relative to the anticipated changes in the exchange rate.

4. In general, the band should be symmetric about the 45° line.

5. These decision models, which are essentially formula approaches to help the firm decide what its exposure should be, should be distinguished from the numerous services which forecast exchange rates. Such forecasts are a necessary component of all decisions about exposure; the other major inputs are the interest agio (or the exchange agio) and the premium required by the firm for becoming exposed.

6. R. B. Shulman, 'Are Foreign Exchange Risks Measurable?', *Columbia Journal of World Business*, v (3) (May–June 1970).

7. Note that the signs of the forecast errors are apparently ignored. Two forecasters might have forecast errors of 20 per cent. Yet one might have an average forecast error of 10 per cent if he is equally wrong on the high side and on the low side 10 per cent of the time, while the other might be on the high side 20 per cent of the time. From the point of view of the firm the second forecaster is more risky.

8. Bernard A. Lietaer, 'Managing Risks in Foreign Exchange', *Harvard Business Review* (Mar–Apr 1970) pp. 127–138, and *Financial Management of Foreign Exchange* (Cambridge, Mass.: MIT Press, 1971).

CHAPTER 12

1. Some firms receive substantially more than 50 per cent of their income from international activities. Since their foreign operations may be levered – their foreign subsidiaries have borrowed dollars – the percentage change in the dollar equivalent of profits on their foreign investments may be substantially larger than the percentage change in the exchange rate.

2. This theory is described in various texts. See William F. Sharpe, *Portfolio Theory and Capital Markets* (New York: McGraw-Hill, 1970).

3. Hence exposure should be calculated following the recommendations of the economist in Chapter 8. If one of the accountant's recommendations is followed, the formal approach to the portfolio may still be followed.

4. Diversification of currency exposures reduces the variance in the firm's income if the deviations from Fisher Open are less than perfectly correlated.

5. In countries other than the United States (as in the United States prior to FASB No. 8) the firm might establish a buffer between exchange losses and gains and its reported income by setting up a reserve which would be credited with exchange gains and perhaps the differential interest income, and charged with exchange losses. The mechanics of establishing the reserve and deciding on the rate at which income will be allocated to the reserve are straightforward. At each moment the firm knows the interest rates at which it might borrow or lend in the several currencies; the amount diverted to the reserve is the product of the interest agio and the exposed position. Reported income – the bottom line – would be insulated from direct changes resulting from changes in exchange rates; the analogy is the bad debt reserves of banks. The firm might then ignore changes in its exposure. Internalising the gains and losses in the variations in the reserve would be deemed less costly than either reporting the variations in income or moving towards a currency mix which minimises variations in reported income by the currently accepted accounting standards.

6. The analysts should be concerned with the apparent persistent bias in the application of Fisher Open; the question is why this bias is not 'competed away'. There may be an apparent market inefficiency – or the apparent deviation may instead represent a payment for political risk.

7. The statement that the firm might alter its exposure to take advantage of anticipated changes in exchange rates makes the prediction of exchange rate changes sound easier than it is. The failure of Herstatt and Franklin National, and the large losses experienced by Lloyds, Banque de Bruxelles and other banks indicates that exchange rate forecasting can be both unsuccessful and costly. Several exchange rate forecasting services are now available; their records are not yet established.

Index